I0793334

Remembering Florence

Tales from a Railroad Town

THOM ANDERSON

THE History PRESS

Published by The History Press
Charleston, SC 29403
www.historypress.net

First published 2009
Second printing 2013

All images from the author's collection unless otherwise noted.

Manufactured in the United States

ISBN 978.1.59629.722.7

Library of Congress Cataloging-in-Publication Data

Anderson, Thom.
Remembering Florence : tales from a railroad town / Thom Anderson.
p. cm.
ISBN 978-1-59629-722-7
1. Florence (S.C.)--History--Anecdotes. 2. Florence (S.C.)--Biography--Anecedotes. I. Title.
F279.F6A49 2009
975.7'84--dc22
2009035283

To my wife, Sandra,
who always gives
at least 100 percent

Contents

Contents

Acknowledgements

I have churned out hundreds, perhaps thousands, of newspaper columns over the years, mostly for the *Morning News* in Florence, and those nearly always have depended on help from somebody, some publication or some institution.

It is the same with this book. The *Morning News* let me use some of the columns I wrote for it over the years, and I greatly appreciate that. Of the new pieces, the *Morning News* files that go back to January 1, 1924, were often used as sources or for confirmation of ideas.

Other newspapers were valuable sources, among them *The State* and the *News and Courier*. Those papers were especially valuable on things that occurred before the *Morning News* existed. Florence newspapers also included the *Florence Evening Star* in the late 1930s and early 1940s, scattered available issues of the *Daily Times*, which shut down in 1925, and others that published briefly. There is much to be found on nineteenth-century Florence in old copies of the *Darlington News* and the *Marion Star*, and I often referred to them. Also, the *Lake City News and Post* and Kingstree weeklies were sources.

The Zeigler Room at the Drs. Bruce and Lee Foundation Florence County Library was my biggest source of help. Ruth Munn Kilgallon and Margaret Collar helped find things and patiently dealt with many dumb questions about operating computers and microfilm machines. Kay Williamson at the Darlington County Historical Commission was very helpful.

The late Dr. G. Wayne King gave me many of the photos back when we often met and marveled at Florence's past, and others were given to me by the late photographer A.W. "Sonny" Smith, with whom I worked at the *Morning News* until his untimely death at age thirty-one.

Our daughter-in-law, Jill W. Anderson, helped me to overcome my ignorance of computers and other modern devices. My wife, Sandra, helped in many ways. So did Suzanne Jebaily, Jumana A. Swindler, Brenda Harrison and Sue Schatz.

Editor Laura All of The History Press was very patient and always reassuring.

Serious histories of the county by Henry Davis, Wayne King and Nick Zeigler served as references and guides. Although this book is a collection of stories about Florence County's past and is not a history, it does touch on county history.

Finally, as with my newspaper columns, the research and collecting of area history by Horace Fraser Rudisill provided the answers to many questions.

Introduction

On January 7, 1853, young Joshua Hudson arrived at the new Florence station on the also new Wilmington and Manchester (W&M) Railroad. Little impressed, he wrote that Florence was "existing only in name, as the only structure was a pine board shed and all else a pine forest."

Where Hudson detrained was the Hoffmeyer Road crossing of the W&M. There, a passenger could connect with a stage line that ran out Hoffmeyer Road toward Darlington. Hudson took that route, winding up in Bennettsville.

The station was named for Florence Henning Harllee, daughter of W.W. Harllee, president of the W&M. Soon, the Florence station moved eastward about two miles to where the North Eastern and Cheraw and Darlington Railroads created a junction with the W&M.

A village that took the name of the station developed around the junction, and soon the Civil War gave it a boost. The junction was important to the Confederate war effort, and refugees came from Charleston. Some became Florentines. A stockade near the village briefly housed Union prisoners late in the war, and a skirmish was fought in Florence with a detachment from Sherman's army. The Confederates won that one.

As the railroads grew in importance, Florence, chartered in 1871, became a small town. Soon there was talk of a new county with Florence as county seat. In late 1888, this happened as parts of Darlington, Marion, Williamsburg and Clarendon Counties made up the new Florence County. The town was re-chartered as a city.

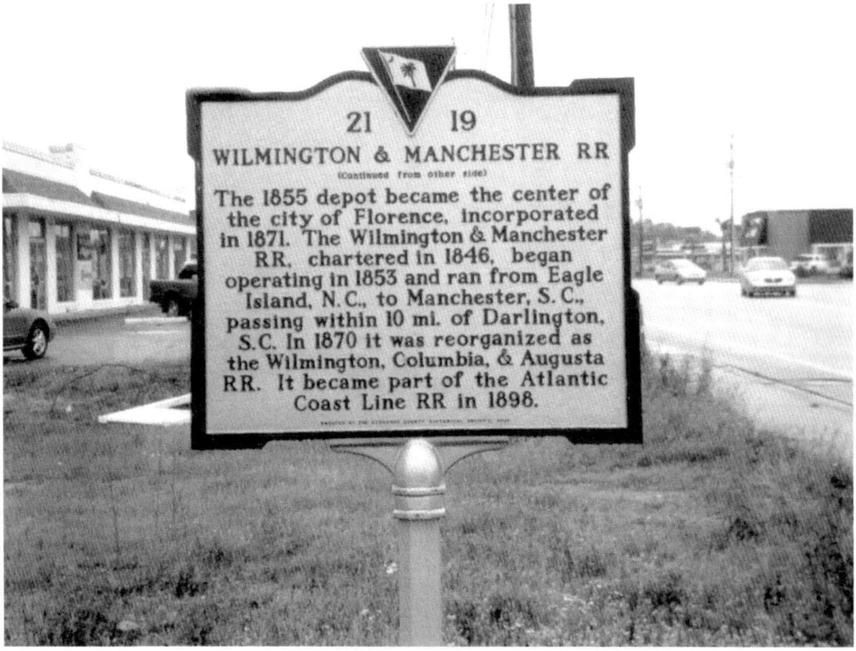

A Hoffmeyer Road plaque in the Florence mall area marks the spot of the first Florence railroad station.

With regional railroad shops, the town prospered, and tobacco soon arrived, boosting the growth of the commercial center of the Pee Dee. Business thrived. Public schools were established. Modern utilities were created.

When the new Florence County dedicated its courthouse in 1890, Joshua Hudson, then a judge living in Bennettsville, was the main speaker. Hudson must have been impressed with the changes that had been brought about since 1853. The site of the Florence station when he first arrived remained forest and farmland, but a couple of miles east, where the Florence station relocated, quite a little city had developed. The business district was modernizing. After fires swept the business area, more modern brick commercial buildings went up along Evans and Dargan Streets where business was re-centering.

The Great Depression slowed growth, but World War II saw an air base here while the war economy boosted Florence out of depression. Industrialization picked up after World War II, and thousands got jobs in plants. Many of those plants eventually moved away or shut down. The railroad declined, and so has tobacco as an income source. Still, local businesses expanded and many flourished.

Urban sprawl came late in the twentieth century. Hudson might get another shock if he were to turn up here again. (He died in 1909, so it's unlikely.) The downtown that he saw developing early in the twentieth century has decayed badly and largely has been razed, much the result of "urban renewal." Sprawl has put most retail businesses miles from the old downtown. Where Hudson detrained in 1853, the pine forests and cultivated fields have mostly vanished, replaced by offices, stores, many bank branches and fast-food places. Now most Florence retail business is near his 1853 arrival point, and a historical marker telling about that station stands where Hoffmeyer Road crossed the railroad. The tracks are gone.

That hits some highlights of a capsule history of Florence, but this is not a history book. It does not need to be. Henry Davis, Wayne King and Nick Zeigler wrote histories of the city and county, detailing how and why the things listed above happened. I am no historian, but I do like stories from Florence history and have retold many over the years in newspaper columns. Some pieces in this book are reprints of old columns. Others are newly written. Included are what I consider good stories, many not important to area development, not the stuff that fills serious histories, so these stories have received little or no space in histories of Florence.

That is the reason for this book. Articles include pieces about the 1958 atomic bomb accident, a Timmonsville man who served for five days as governor, a well-planned Lake City bank robbery, a governor and a circuit judge in a fistfight at the Florence Courthouse, a seventeen-inch snowfall and others. Although things that did not figure greatly in the overall development of the city and county are included, they are worth telling and retelling. Serious historians have served up the meat and potatoes of Florence history. This is sort of dessert.

This book, in its own way, is informative and, I hope, entertaining.

A City Named for Her

William Wallace Harllee was reading a Dickens novel named *Dombey and Son* in 1848 when his first daughter was born. He liked the book's character named Florence, and he gave his daughter that name.

A few years later, Harllee was president of the Wilmington and Manchester Railroad, which was being constructed from Wilmington, North Carolina, to the Sumter County village of Manchester. The rural depot where Hoffmeyer Road crossed the W&M right of way was named Florence in Harllee's daughter's honor. The settlement—later village and still later town—that developed around the junction took the name of the depot, and eventually a new county took the name of Florence.

Florence Henning Harllee grew up in the Mars Bluff community and then moved with her family to Marion. Later, they moved again to a Florence house at Irby and Pine Streets. Florence, who never married, apparently had a strong will and perhaps a bit of eccentricity. A great-niece wrote about her that Florence and her unmarried sister, Lizzie, shared the Florence home after their parents' death, but each maintained what practically amounted to separate residences. The house had a hall down the middle that led into a parlor that the sisters shared for entertaining, but each had a side of the house to herself, including separate kitchens.

About 1970, Virginia Ravenel wrote that Florence and Lizzie taught school and had other enterprises to make money. Florence Harllee was the librarian in 1903 when the Florence Civic Improvement Society established a public library in the city hall. When interest in a public library was sufficient

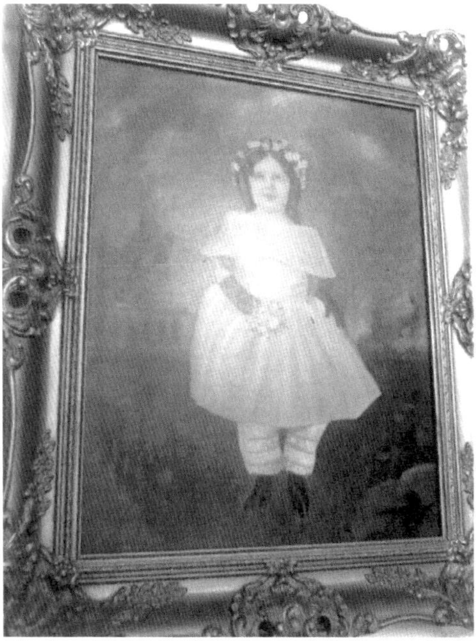

Florence Harllee as a child. *Courtesy of Wayne King.*

for tax support, a building was planned. The Harllee sisters' property at Irby and Pine was purchased, and the Florence Public Library was built there. It remained there about eighty years until moving into the Drs. Bruce and Lee Library on South Dargan.

The community that bore her name apparently sought to honor her more than she wanted to be honored. When, in the early 1920s, Florence and Marion had a celebration to open the first highway bridge between the counties, plans were begun to make her guest of honor. She and her niece and great-niece, all named Florence, were invited. While the nieces were pleased, Florence Harllee scoffed at the idea of "making a spectacle of ourselves" and declined the invitation.

She might also have scoffed at this, but when she died on May 5, 1927, Mayor H.K. Gilbert issued a proclamation asking all businesses to close during her funeral. The city bell tolled at that hour. *The State* newspaper reported that "great throngs of Florence people will gather at the church and at the country graveyard to pay their last respects."

She was buried beside her father in the Hopewell Presbyterian Church graveyard at Claussen.

Murder and Hanging

About five men went into a store near Florence in 1869 for a robbery that went bad. It led to a hanging that was feared might lead to racial strife.

On January 10, 1869, the men entered the store of M.A. Muldrow. Robert Suggs, the lone clerk at the time, was killed. The robbers were black and the store clerk was white. According to the *Camden Journal*, from their nearby home Suggs's wife heard gunshots, and an armed neighbor came to help. The robbers fired on him, and two bystanders were wounded. There was much agitation, and a manhunt was launched. Cyrus Coachman, one of the robbers, was caught. Testimony at the trial said that much of the merchandise stolen from the store was found in and around Coachman's home.

The Darlington jail had burned down, so Coachman was jailed in Marion to await trial. The *Marion Star* covered the Darlington trial and its aftermath. At that time, Florence was located in Darlington County.

Edward Jackson, another black man, also was charged, but he had an alibi that stood up, and he was acquitted. Coachman was found guilty and sentenced to hang. Governor Robert Scott, the first Reconstruction-era governor, delayed the execution to review the case, and Coachman apparently expected Scott to save him.

Scott reviewed the record provided by Judge Rutland, which showed that Suggs had been murdered by one of five men who robbed the store. The stolen goods found in Coachman's possession "in his house and about it" Coachman claimed to have bought from some other men. The record showed that Suggs was murdered by one of five men, and Coachman was one of the five, according to witnesses. It was argued that even if Coachman did not fire the fatal shots, he was "present, aided and abetted."

"Judge Rutland describes Coachman as having a bad face, and the homicide was a most daring, unprovoked and premeditated act," the *Star* reported. The judge stated that Coachman was "well-defended" and that he was "convicted upon Negro evidence and a jury partly colored."

One witness identified Jackson as the shooter, but upon seeing Jackson and Coachman together, changed his testimony and said that Coachman fired the shots.

Governor Scott declined to interfere, so the execution was scheduled for Friday, June 18, 1869, between 10:00 a.m. and 5:00 p.m. in Darlington. Coachman was brought from Marion to temporary quarters in Darlington the day before.

Sheriff T.C. Cox was black, as were many of those carrying out the execution. Since there was fear that an attempt would be made by local blacks to rescue Coachman, Cox deputized a large group of citizens, divided between black and white, to keep order. One source said that there were seventy special deputies, forty white and thirty black, all well armed. That force was commanded by Cox and Deputies John W. Lee (white) and Joe Cavin (black). Thankfully, there was no trouble at the execution.

On Thursday night and Friday morning, Coachman reportedly told different stories, but on Friday, Captain E.K. Dargan, defense attorney, said that Coachman confessed, describing the crime and naming accomplices. Dargan described Coachman's confession: Charles Howe was said to have organized the crime. The *Star* described Howe as "an intelligent mulatto rascal…who was formerly a deputy sheriff and one of the principal witnesses for the state."

Coachman named five others involved, saying that he and one other were not armed. He said that the fatal shots were fired from outside when Coachman and one other refused to shoot. Then goods were thrown through a window and carried away. Each accomplice gave a share of his goods to the ringleader, who was said to have advised that the stolen items be hidden. The others named by Coachman apparently fled and later took new names.

The *Star* said that about 500 blacks and 150 whites turned up at the gallows erected beside the jail. About 3:00 p.m., Coachman was marched to the gallows, led by four men carrying a coffin. Coachman was dressed in a white robe and stockinged feet, accompanied by three black clergymen who led the singing of hymns. The sentence and confession were read, and Coachman made his mark on the document.

At 4:20 p.m., he climbed onto the scaffold and asked the crowd to sing "Hark to the Tombs a Doleful Sound, May Ears Attend the Cry." Reverend E.M. Pinckney, one of the clergymen, prayed, and the preachers led another hymn as the rope was placed around the prisoner's neck. Coachman spoke and asked people to tell his wife to meet him in heaven and said again that he had not committed the murder.

At 4:25 p.m., a deputy cut the rope and Coachman fell, breaking his neck. The body was given to friends for burial.

Witnesses said that, to the end, Coachman apparently had expected rescue. They said that whenever he heard a noise, he turned, beaming, expecting to be saved.

Years later, one of the accomplices, then going under the name of McKay, was caught, tried, convicted and also hanged.

Florence in the 1890s

Morning News column, February 16, 2003

So you think local boards and commissions have done things to make you miserable? What if all males in Florence between the ages of sixteen and fifty were required to put in three to six days of work on the streets each May or another time, as might be set by the city council? And if any person failed to perform this labor, the intendant would "cause the marshal to bring the offending party before him to be dealt with according to the law."

That was how it was here in the 1890s, part of what I found in a photocopy of an 1892 Florence directory of "Merchants, Manufacturers, General Industries, Professional and Leading Businessmen." It is one of the goodies residing at the Florence County Library.

Getting back to street work duty, the directory says that firemen, school trustees, the intendant and wardens (similar to mayor and council) and "regularly ordained ministers of the Gospel" were excused.

Florence had just been re-chartered as a city a couple of years before this directory, believed to be the city's first, was published. It contains some interesting information about Florence as it was then. Included are drawings of the old courthouse in its original state with a tower, looking a little like a church, and the first city hall, a two-story frame building with a porch, facing Evans Street. It was on the same site as the later city hall, which, when the city moved into the City-County Complex in the 1970s, was improved into eighteen parking places.

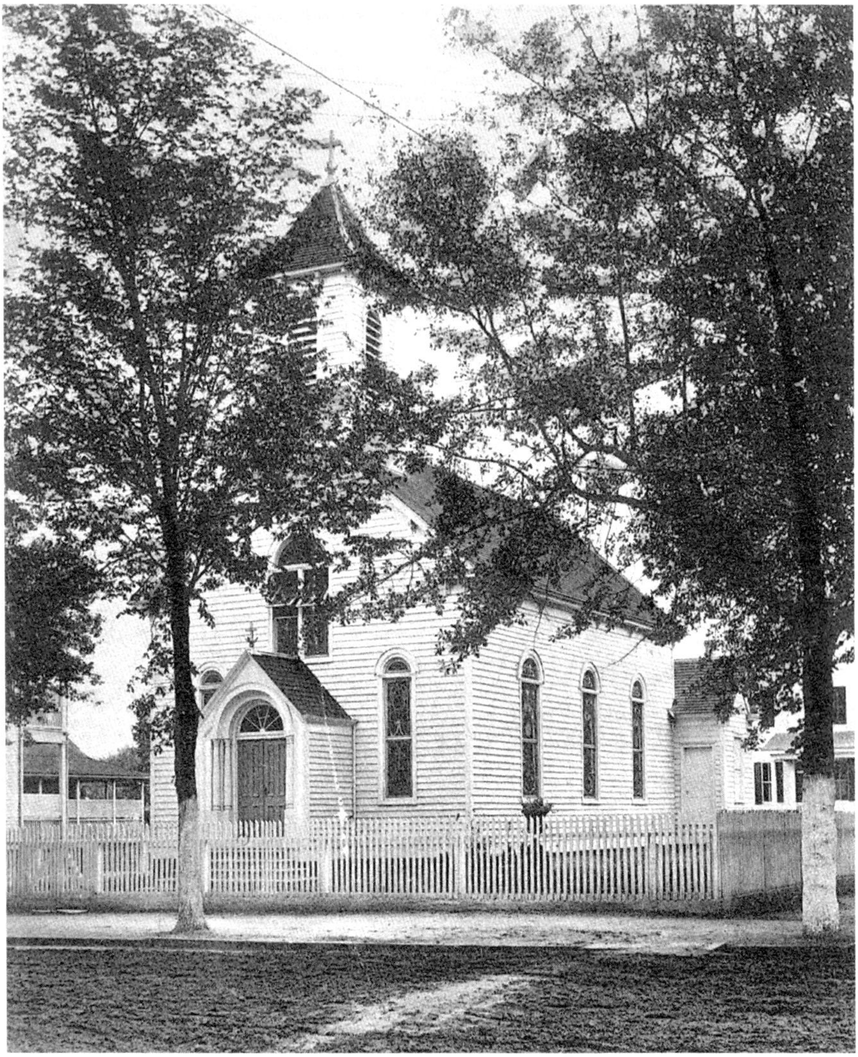

St. Anthony Catholic Mission on an old postcard.

Besides the narrative about the city, there are also many ads for local businesses, none of which are still here. There was Emporium! (the exclamation point was part of the shop's name), which was opposite the post office, then on North Dargan Street. The post office at Evans and Irby was still more than a decade in the future. The shop offered "fashionable millinery, fancy and imported goods, latest French styles."

Jerome P. Chase was mayor and D.J. Justice, Dr. F.D. Covington, W.J. Bradford and W.J. Brown were wardens.

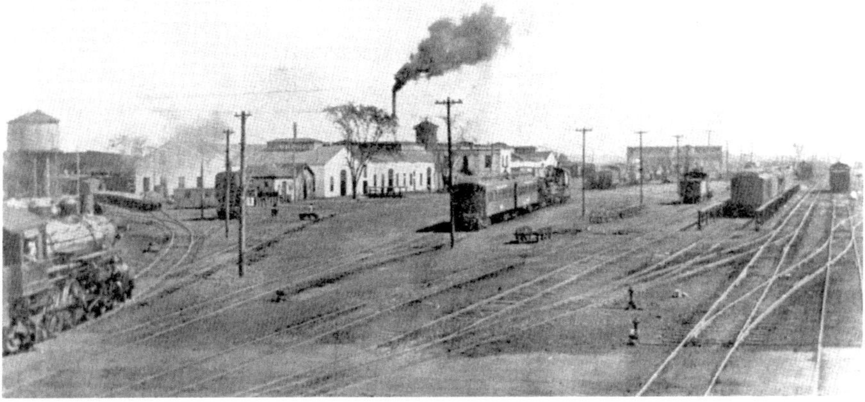

Early view of Florence's ACL Railroad yard. *Courtesy of Wayne King*

I'll tell you one thing: John P. Coffin a busy fellow. The directory says that he was president of a bank, a building and loan, a laundry and a wood and coal yard. He was representative of an insurance company, vice-president of a real estate company and financial manager of a brick-making firm and mattress factory.

Getting back to a local council messing with you, here are some local laws published in the directory: "After 10 o'clock at night, all clamorous singing, whooping or other obstreperous, wanton and unnecessary noises calculated to disturb the peace and quiet of the city are hereby prohibited on pain of $5 or imprisonment not exceeding 10 days."

It goes on to explain that the law did not apply to "decent and decorous" dancing, "but exclusively to disorderly houses or places which are frequented by women of ill-fame and others associating with them, or by disorderly persons." Heavens! Do you suppose there really was such activity in Florence?

Sunday behavior was expected to be a cut above weekdays. There was a fifty-dollar fine for disturbing church or being drunk in church, but doesn't it seem that somebody who was drunk on Sunday morning needed the attention of a church? People on horseback or vehicles were forbidden to pass a church at a speed faster than a normal walking pace.

One ad said that a local business was the "only all-night house in the city for the sale of wines, liquors, tobacco and cigars." It was near the Atlantic Coast Line passenger station, which at the time was located under the present Church Street bridge.

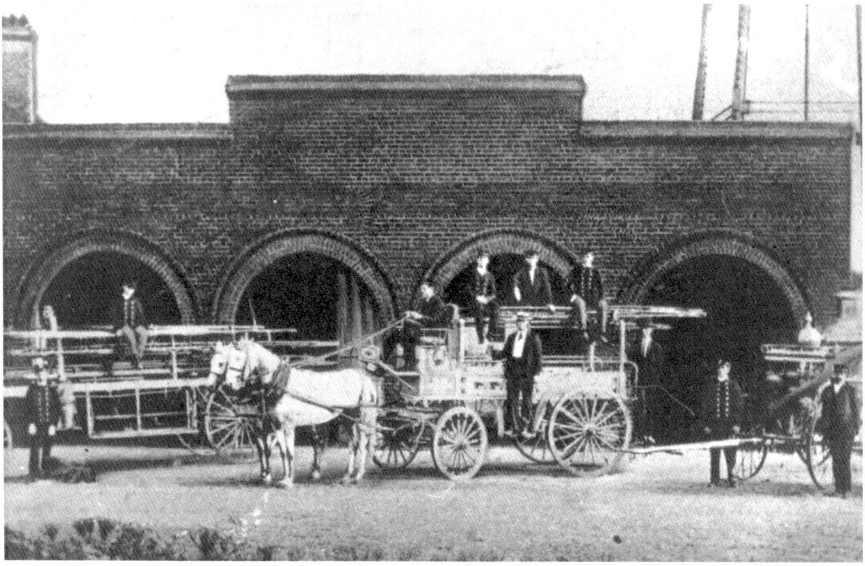

Old Florence Fire Department on Front Street. *Courtesy of Wayne King.*

Forty-four trains came through daily, the directory said, and there were four newspapers: the *Times*, the *Messenger*, the *Centenary* and the *Baptist Herald*. The *Morning News* was still about a quarter-century away.

There were no autos, of course, but modernity was creeping up on Florence. The Florence Improvement and Investment Co. had put $35,000 in "an electric light plant," and electricity was becoming available to public buildings and private residences.

There was a macadamized road to the National Cemetery, and one could stay at the Commercial Hotel for one dollar a night. If that's too steep, they had special rates for regular boarders.

That's a look at Florence near the end of the nineteenth century. What do you suppose folks in 2113 will think of us?

Florence in Insurrection?

Florence County once was declared in rebellion by the governor. It grew out of the Darlington Riot of 1894. Resentment of Governor Benjamin Tillman's dispensary system, a state alcohol monopoly, was high. State officers were closing illegal saloons—or "blind tigers"—and some of the press inflamed the population, calling the state agents Tillman's "spies" and the dispensary law "iniquitous."

It came to a head in Darlington on March 30, 1894, when a fight broke out between two young men that developed into a riot and shootout. A dispensary agent and two Darlington men died, and others were wounded.

While Darlington seethed and crowds blamed the dispensary agents, whom the press branded "murderers," Florence, ten miles away, seethed in sympathy with Darlington. "At this writing, trouble is feared in Florence," read a news report on March 31.

A mob broke into the Florence dispensary, trashed it and poured about $15,000 worth of booze into gutters. "Everybody is pleased to know that Florence now has no dispensary," a newspaper reported, adding, "Whiskey is flowing in the gutters, and even the colored people refuse to drink it." The Timmonsville dispensary also was looted. Besides the attack on the dispensary, weapons and ammunition of the Florence Rifles militia unit reportedly were taken by a mob. It seemed likely that guns were going to vigilantes.

Enraged people around Florence were threatening to become vigilantes and hunt dispensary agents who had escaped a Darlington crowd and retreated into the woods. Lynching was threatened because of the assumption that Tillman would pardon the agents if they were tried and convicted.

Vigilantes from Florence and Darlington scoured a rural area near Hoffmeyer Road where "spies" reportedly had been seen. It was assumed that sympathetic people in the area would help them. Also, news reports claimed that Tillman supporters around Timmonsville were arming themselves and preparing to help the threatened agents. At one point, armed Tillman supporters in Timmonsville were said to have left town in buggies, presumably to help the "spies." It was feared that Tillmanite and anti-Tillman forces might fight one another in military-like units.

Once it was believed that dispensary agents were aboard a freight train en route from Darlington, and about fifty armed men waited in Florence. The Florence sheriff "demanded peace in the name of the law," but the crowd paid little attention. They instructed a flagman to tell the agents to surrender or be shot. All were ready as the train arrived, but no "spies" were aboard. Disappointed vigilantes then formed squads to search the countryside for "spies."

J.S. McKenzie, a potential candidate for postmaster, was believed to be helping Tillman's agents. A quick protest was sent to Washington, D.C., against his possible appointment.

A special train from Florence to Darlington carried men pledged to help Darlington. They met with Darlington people and, together with a Sumter delegation, passed resolutions pledging to protect one another's homes "from unreasonable searches and to resist arrests if attempted to be made by spies."

Unrest was sufficient that Tillman declared Florence and Darlington Counties in insurrection. The governor's resolution read that elements of the population in Florence and Darlington "are now in open rebellion against the authority of this state and it has become impracticable to enforce by the ordinary course of judicial proceedings the laws of this state in said counties." The governor declared them in open rebellion and said, "I do hereby command all such assemblages of insurgents to disperse and retire peaceable to their respective abodes."

Probably most important to the governor was that the insurrection declaration gave the state authority to seize and operate the railroads and telegraph lines through Florence. It also authorized martial law.

Cooler was W.W. Harllee, former president of the first area railroad. As a lawyer, he said that Tillman had violated the law but urged citizens, if arrested, to submit under protest. As state militia moved into Florence, Harllee said that members of the militia would be subject to prosecution if they violated private rights.

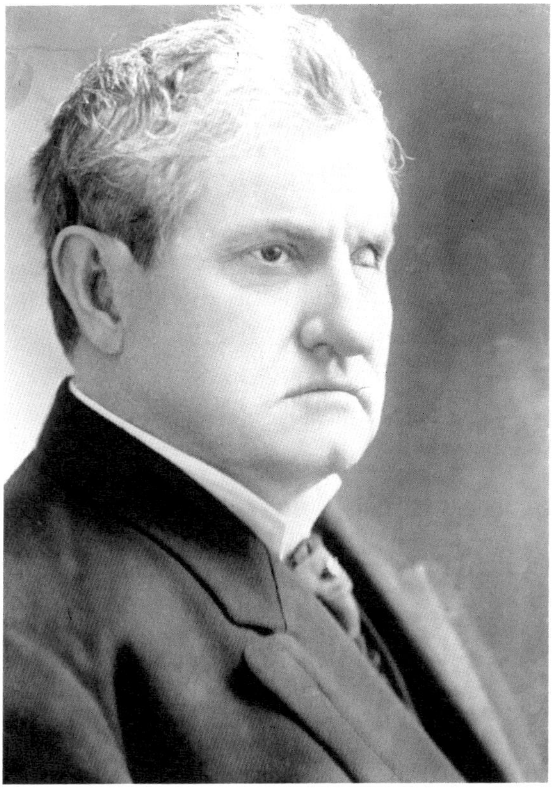

Governor Benjamin Tillman. *Courtesy of the Library of Congress.*

Tillman, who had been elected in a heated and divisive campaign, had some militia units refuse his orders to go to Darlington and Florence to keep order. Finally, many of his rural supporters came as a new militia.

Despite the heated emotions and possibility of much bloodshed, things calmed down pretty quickly in Florence, probably because they calmed down in Darlington, the center of it all. When Tillman's militia arrived in Florence, it was pretty quiet. The units were from Greenwood, Clinton, Edgefield and Elloree. One news report said that among them was Jim Tillman, the governor's nephew, who later would become lieutenant governor. Adjutant General Farley made his headquarters in Florence.

When the militia units arrived, they marched through Evans Street and were "drawn up" in front of the Central Hotel. They were housed in the Florence Rifles armory and fed in the Central Hotel.

All was not friendly, though. A dispensary agent turned up in Florence and attempted to register at the Central Hotel. He was ordered out by the proprietor.

By April 1, things were so quiet in Florence that all factions peaceably mingled, and the declaration of insurrection was considered "a huge joke by the grimmest of jokers." The *News and Courier* reported that "only two fist fights were attempted, both of which were nipped in the bud."

The Florence clerk of court received orders to organize troops faithful to the state government, but he would not attempt it. The sheriff was ordered to send deputies to disperse vigilantes, but he did not. All was quiet already.

On April 5, all was quiet in Darlington and therefore in Florence. When militia units reached Florence, all trouble appeared to have cooled, and their members seemed to have enjoyed their Florence visit. An Edgefield unit said the day before that they planned to "leave tomorrow with nothing but good will for the people of Florence, outlaws though they may be."

The militia units staged a formal parade in Florence the day before leaving. Adjutant General Farley thanked the community for its reception, and Major Wardlaw proposed "three cheers for Florence," which was done. One of the Santee Rifles said that he liked the place so much that he planned to return to Florence to live. On their march to the train, the militiamen gave three cheers for the Central Hotel.

If there was ill feeling left between the towns because of the formation of Florence County having cost Darlington County some territory, perhaps the support of one for the other soothed that.

On April 17, the Darlington City Council passed a resolution thanking neighboring communities "and particularly…our sister city of Florence for the disinterested and timely aid rendered us during the severe ordeal through which we have recently passed."

Years later, a Darlington woman's diary on the events was published, and at one point she wrote that there was also trouble in Florence. "Hope Florence is not suffering. Hope our people will help her. The little town will always help us; came up when they heard we were suffering."

Rowdy Campaigners

An exciting headline in July 1896 read, "A Fisticuff Between Earle and Evans at Florence." It must have been quite a night at the old Florence County Courthouse when the candidates for statewide office met during a "stump meeting." They appeared together at all county seats and debated the issues before the Democratic primary.

Candidates for a U.S. Senate seat were Governor John Gary Evans, one of Ben Tillman's closest allies, who had succeeded him as governor; Judge Joseph H. Earle, conservative with whom Evans was staging a very bitter debate; and John T. Duncan, a Newberry man who mainly wanted to thwart Evans.

Campaigns in the young county had been rather rowdy in the past, and the meetings became more and more heated as the tour progressed. Earlier, Earle felt that Evans's attacks became too personal and was said to have warned the governor that Evans would continue the attacks at his peril.

According to newspaper reports, Earle was the first of the Senate candidates to speak and mostly dealt with national issues. Then Evans and Earle exchanged comments about questions that had arisen earlier in Lancaster. Things seemed to have calmed, and then Evans made a remark that seemed to refer to "fice dogs with their tails cut." Fice dogs apparently referred to mongrels, perhaps little, loud, excitable mongrels.

Earle, who was seated about five or six feet from where Evans spoke before the judge's bench, approached the governor. He said that the remarks went too far and asked Evans, "Do you refer to me?" The governor gave a little rather dismissive wave of the hand, saying that his remarks hurt nobody.

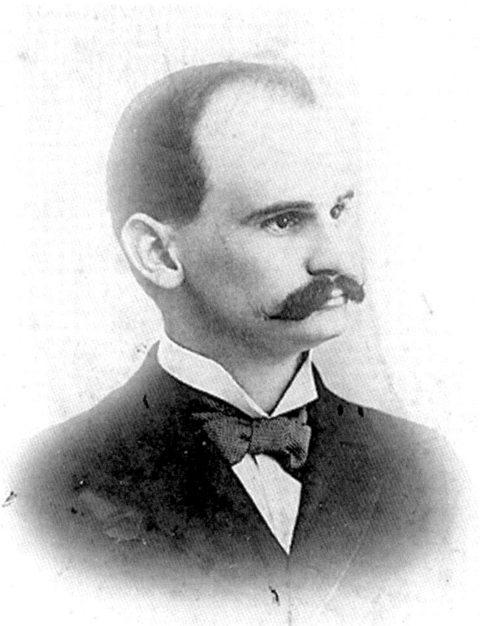

Governor John Gary Evans. *Courtesy of the Library of Congress.*

"What did you mean?" Earle demanded.

Evans responded, "I mean just what I said, that you and Duncan are going around like two little fice dogs."

Earle then struck at Evans, who ducked and, according to newspapers, was hit in the head and back if at all. They clinched, and blows were delivered before some of the crowd separated them. Sheriff McLendon and a couple of others pulled Earle away. Chairman McCall and others pulled Evans away. Then several men stood between them. Evans, on a slightly elevated platform, was described as "pale with excitement" but without bruises. Earle had blood trickling down his face.

It appeared that more of Evans's friends were around him, but it quickly evened up as Earle supporters gathered. Some apparently wanted to join the fight, but there was "more talking than anything else." It was a moment that could have been tragic. Pistols were drawn, but none were fired. W.E. Gonzales wrote in *The State* newspaper that "pistols were drawn by that class of men who do not feel safe without a gun in their hands. Some were calling for blood and some for peace."

With drawn pistols in the middle of a fierce argument, Florence was lucky that night not to have experienced a tragedy that would have stained its history and reputation.

Judging by applause, the three hundred in the courtroom were about evenly divided between Evans and Earle supporters. Apparently lost in the confusion were arguments about handling of alcohol and insurance contracts, which were big issues that year.

As things cooled, Earle mounted a chair, saying, "The thing is over and let everybody sit down, and I am sorry for it." Then Evans shouted that it was over and asked his friends to sit down and be quiet.

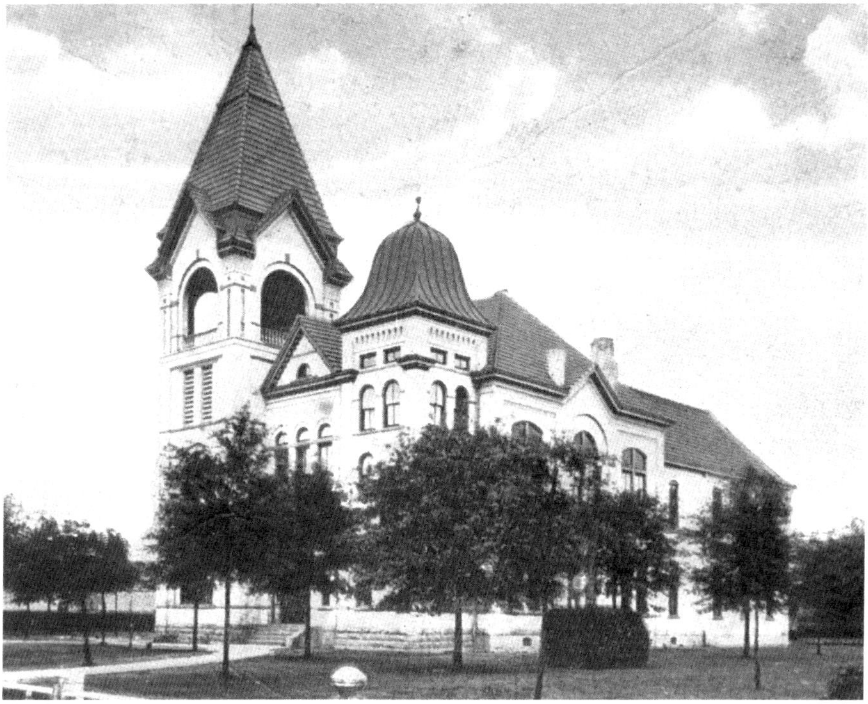

The first Florence Courthouse, where campaigners scrapped. *Courtesy of Wayne King.*

Evans began to speak again, but cheering for one candidate or another interrupted. Responding to hisses, August Kohn of the *News and Courier* wrote that Evans said they were "a little coterie of town boys and he was going to cram something down their throats as Tillman had done in the dispensary matter." [This was a reference to when Tillman had sent militia to Florence in that crisis; see previous article for full story.]

A "Mr. Swails" warned Evans to be careful about what he had to say about "these town fellows."

His turn, Duncan made charges against Evans that were "particularly vehement and scathing."

Reporters covering the stump series seemed to enjoy contrasting the behavior of the candidates and their supporters with what was widely believed to be the proper theme of the campaign—education. One report noted that 45 percent of South Carolinians could not read, broken down as 17 percent of whites and 64 percent of blacks.

Kohn wrote that "if the people of Florence are properly judged, they very likely went away from this meeting with very much more disgust than satisfaction."

Gonzales wrote that "it was a shocking scene for a South Carolinian to contemplate, but it was the culmination of practices upon the stump that have heretofore been disgraceful." *The State* commented editorially, "This affair will probably end the primary system. It ought to."

Evans and Earle supporters argued afterward over who got the better of the fisticuffs. Although Earle apparently was the only one who lost blood, his supporters argued that the blow was thrown by a young man who jumped into the fray. Evans was confident that he had struck Earle.

Afterward, the mayor issued a warrant for Evans and Earle for something like disturbing the peace. Earle posted a ten-dollar bond, which he planned to forfeit. Then the chief of police went to serve the warrant on the governor, who was visiting relatives in town. Evans treated the warrants as a joke, saying, probably quite correctly, that he would first have to be impeached. The police chief then returned Earle's bond payment.

Since Earle was the only one who shed blood, Evans might be called the winner of the Florence sideshow, but in the main event he was a loser. Evans got more than 49 percent of the vote in the primary, missing a majority by 617 votes. Duncan, whose only goal was denying the governor a majority, was successful. In a runoff, Earle won with 52 percent while carrying Florence County.

Earle took his Senate seat in May 1897 but died on May 20, 1897, and the seat was up for grabs again. Evans tried three more times for the Senate but never made it.

Evans and Earle had served in both houses of the legislature. Evans was elected governor in 1894, the same year that Earle became a circuit judge. Evans lived until 1942.

Don't Disrespect Robert E. Lee

Like many public spaces in the South after the Civil War, the Jacobi House lobby in Florence had a portrait of General Robert E. Lee in an honored place. A couple of salesmen from the North learned one night in the 1890s that it paid, if one could not show respect for the beloved Confederate general, at least not to show blatant disrespect.

The Jacobi was near the Florence railroad station, where Front (now Baroody) Street crossed Church Street. A local police duty then was to escort late-arriving train passengers to the hotels. One night, J. Crog Brunson, a local cop and Confederate army veteran, escorted passengers. When they entered the Jacobi, the salesmen spotted the Lee portrait. Apparently wanting to remind South Carolinians within hearing distance who won the war, they made fun of the picture.

With Brunson there, this was a big mistake. At the lobby desk, he ceremonially removed his badge, gun and other police equipment and then announced that he would now act as a private citizen. It is unclear whether Brunson dealt with both salesmen or just the more offensive one. Anyway, if he only attacked one, the other seemed uninterested in challenging the enraged policeman. At least one of the salesmen got a good beating, so if his side won the war thirty years earlier, he lost this skirmish.

The next day, the bruised salesman protested to the mayor and demanded satisfaction. The mayor called an emergency meeting of the city council and had Brunson appear. It must have been much like at court. Council members got descriptions of the incident, questioned participants and then

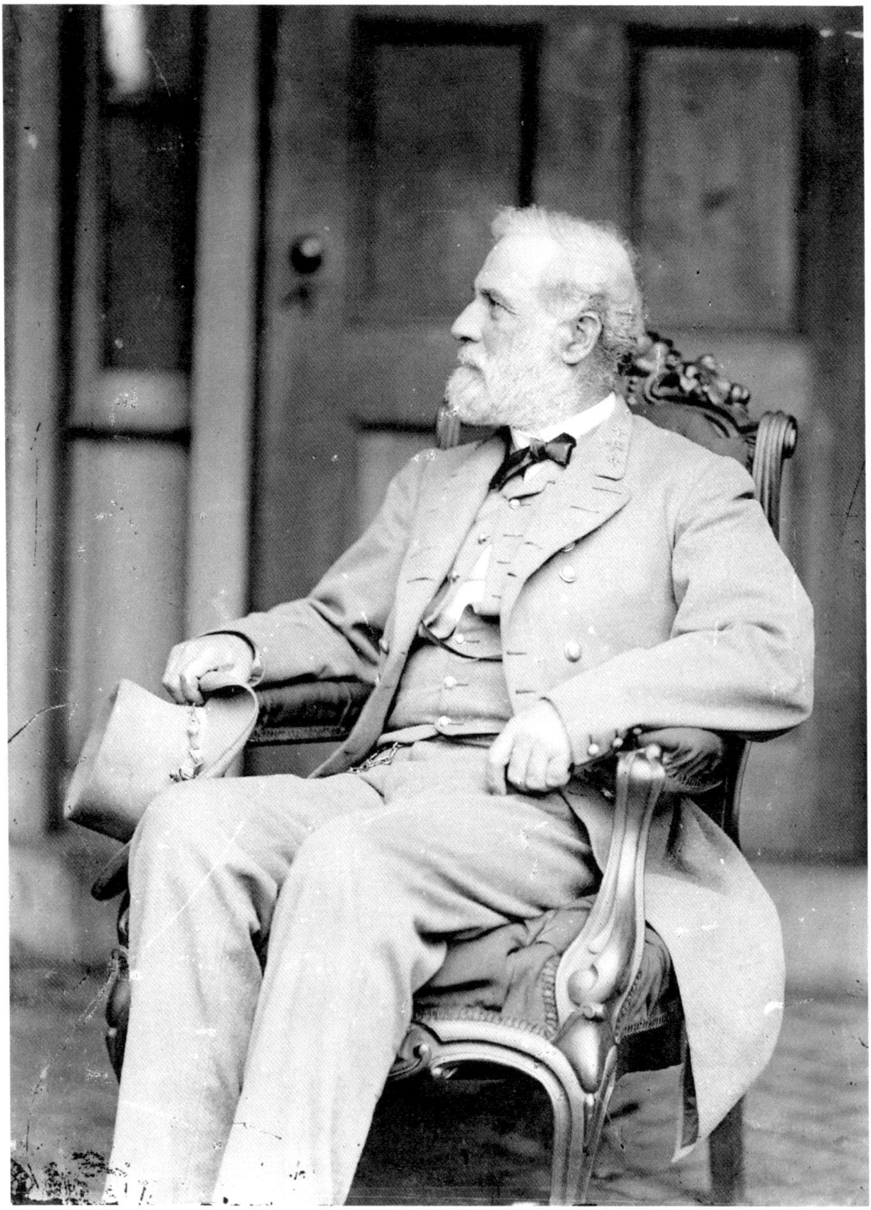

Robert E. Lee. *Courtesy of the Library of Congress.*

withdrew to consider the evidence. Finally, they called Brunson up and, as it is told, pronounced him guilty of splendid performance of duty and gave him a nice pay raise and some vacation time. The salesmen's reaction does not seem to have been recorded.

Brunson, like many at that time, had a fierce loyalty to Lee and to the defeated Confederacy. Before becoming a Florence cop, Brunson had served as a law officer in Darlington County and was one of three elected to a four-man Florence police force by the city council in May 1898, according to Wayne King's history of Florence County. He apparently served as a local health officer after his police career.

The *Dillon Herald* carried an obituary after Crog Brunson's death on October 31, 1916. The first paragraph read, "Mr. J. Crog Brunson, another of Florence's old and best known citizens and a Confederate veteran, passed to the great beyond shortly after six o'clock yesterday afternoon." It reported that he had not been feeling well for several days "but was able to be up and around."

"Yesterday he was uptown and late in the afternoon went to his home on South Warley Street. He retired soon after reaching his home and a short time afterwards his wife went to his room to see after him and found that life was extinct," the obit read.

The funeral service would await the arrival of his son, Norment Brunson, from Helena, Arkansas, but would be at his residence, with burial in Mount Hope Cemetery.

Mount Hope Cemetery

Morning News column, September 28, 2003

Going into Mount Hope Cemetery, one passes an obelisk and a Confederate flag. It is the Confederate monument that once stood at the original First Presbyterian Church on Church Street. When the monument was placed on the church grounds in 1882, Florence was not a county seat, so there were no courthouse grounds. It was placed where about sixty-four Confederate soldiers had been buried during the Civil War. They had died here at a makeshift rail-side hospital.

When the church moved to the 100 block of East Evans in 1906, the adjoining graveyard was abandoned. The soldiers' bodies were moved to Mount Hope Cemetery, which a few years earlier had been established on the town's southern outskirts. The monument was moved with them and placed above the common grave of the soldiers, according to Wayne King's and Nick Zeigler's histories of Florence County. A number of other graves from the old Presbyterian churchyard and the old Fraternal Burying Ground on East Pine Street were also moved to Mount Hope in its early years.

A cemetery is a good place to get in touch with a community's past. It calls to mind many stories about people who were buried there. Perhaps the most famous inhabitant of Mount Hope is Melvin Purvis, the FBI agent who led the agents who pursued and finally shot John Dillinger to death in Chicago when Dillinger was Public Enemy Number One. Purvis came out of Timmonsville and was a lawyer before joining the Bureau. It is said that the G-

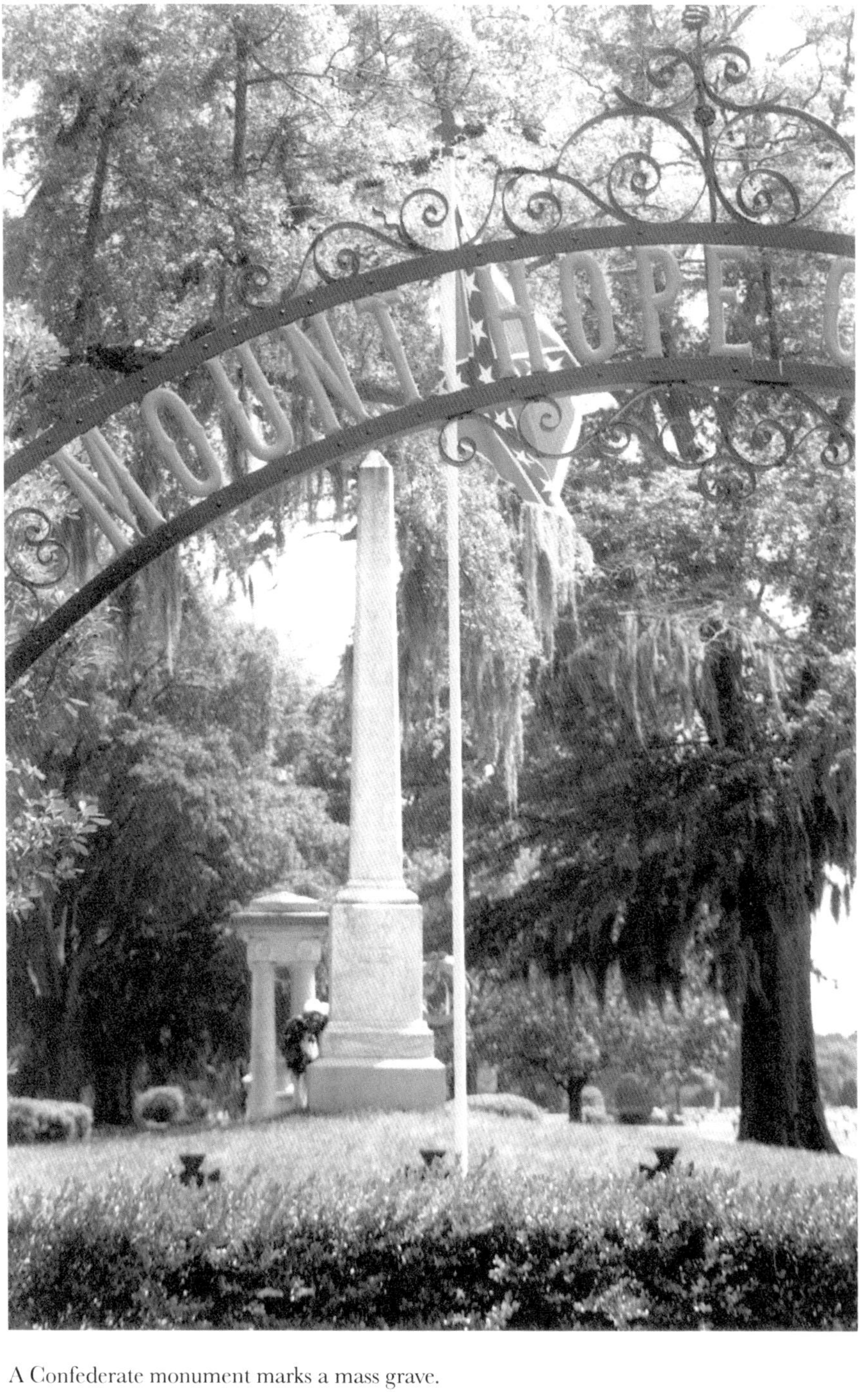

A Confederate monument marks a mass grave.

man designation grew out of Purvis's fame as a "government man." After he left the FBI (it also is said that he was pushed out because J. Edgar Hoover was jealous of Purvis's fame), Purvis did other government service and then came back to Florence, published a newspaper and owned a radio station.

Four members of Congress are also buried at Mount Hope. J. Willard Ragsdale was from Timmonsville and practiced law in Florence, starting in 1898. He served in the South Carolina legislature. In 1912, he was the first Florence County resident elected to Congress, in which he served until he died in office in 1919.

Allard H. Gasque was Florence County superintendent of education when he resigned in 1923 after having been elected to Congress. He served until he died in office in 1938. Elizabeth Hawley Gasque, his widow, was elected to the remaining months of Gasque's term and served as Sixth District congresswoman from September 13, 1938, until January 3, 1939. She died at age 103 and was one of the oldest people buried at Mount Hope.

Following her was John L. McMillan, who was elected to Congress in 1938 and served until early 1973. He first was buried in Mullins but, several years later, was moved to Mount Hope.

A chief justice of the state supreme court was buried there. D. Gordon Baker was a Florence lawyer and legislator who later served for twenty-one

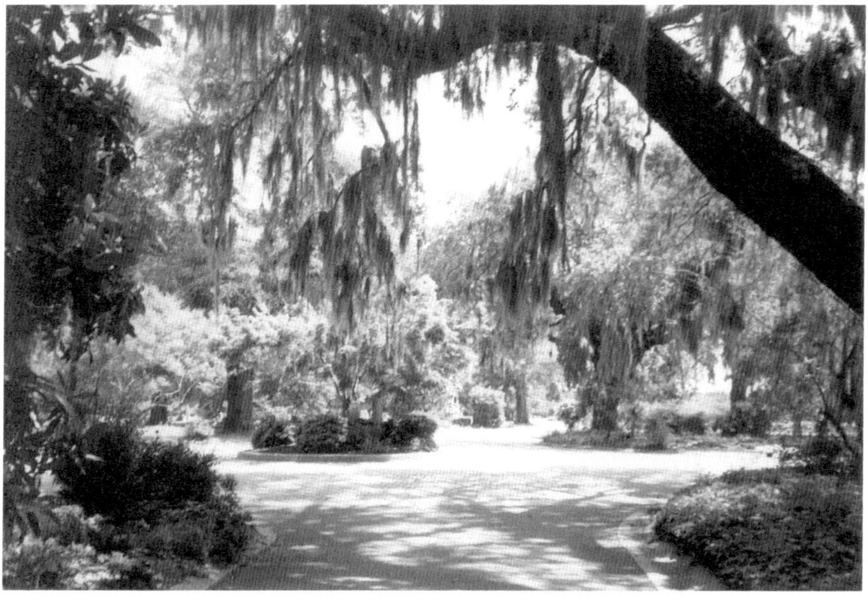

The main entrance road into Florence's Mount Hope Cemetery.

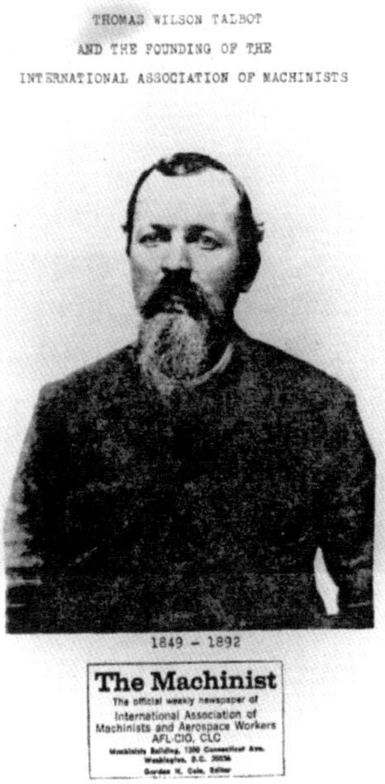

Thomas William Talbot.

years on the South Carolina Supreme Court, twelve of those as chief justice.

In a strongly anti-union area, it might be surprising to find the gravesite and monument to Thomas Wilson Talbot, who is credited with founding the United Machinists and Mechanical Engineers of America union. Talbot worked in Florence railroad shops, where he organized a small local union and got fired as a result. Later, he organized a chapter elsewhere, which grew into the national union. Then he ran a Florence machine shop. The union put up a ten-foot-high obelisk at his Mount Hope grave and also mounted a statue of Talbot in Atlanta.

The first burial in the cemetery, which was then outside the southern borders of the town, was that of Kate Coe Brunson Hamby, who died on January 5, 1883. The earliest death date is 1836. That was John McGown, whose grave was one of those moved to Mount Hope when other cemeteries were abandoned. The Confederate monument is not the only war memorial on the grounds. A garden club also placed a memorial to local people who died in World War II.

After about 120 years, Mount Hope must be a good operation. It never has had a complaint from any of its residents. Manager Sara Moseley said that about fifteen thousand people are buried there. Among them are most mayors, many city council members, legislators and other names prominent in local history. I found many of my old teachers and principals there. It's a nice place to walk around and think.

Florence Railroad Stations

Florence railroad stations have turned up in literature and have had very famous and not famous people visit them at one time or another. The earliest recorded visit was in 1853, when Joshua H. Hudson was going to a teaching job in Bennettsville. In his memoir, he described arriving at the Florence station that January 7. The station at which Hudson arrived was where Hoffmeyer Road crossed the Wilmington and Manchester Railroad and was no more than a shed near the present Florence Mall. Soon, a junction was established, and the Florence station moved to where the downtown is now. Later Florence stations were from Coit Street to Day Street.

The Florence station appears in Mary Boykin Chesnut's famous Civil War diary. Her husband, General J.C. Chesnut, disembarked from the train in Florence for coffee and was left behind. Mrs. Chesnut had adventures before finally getting to their home in Camden.

The most famous of southerners, Robert E. Lee, changed trains three times in Florence. The first was early in the Civil War when he was going to lead the defense of Charleston and was not yet the object of near worship. Then he passed again on his return to Virginia, where he took command of the main Confederate army.

He might not have created much of a stir on those occasions, but he must have when he made his final long trip in 1871. Headed northward after a tour of the South, Lee was met by a delegation from Wilmington that brought a special train to carry him to that city. Cadets from a Wilmington school formed for review, but according to one biographer, Lee went to the

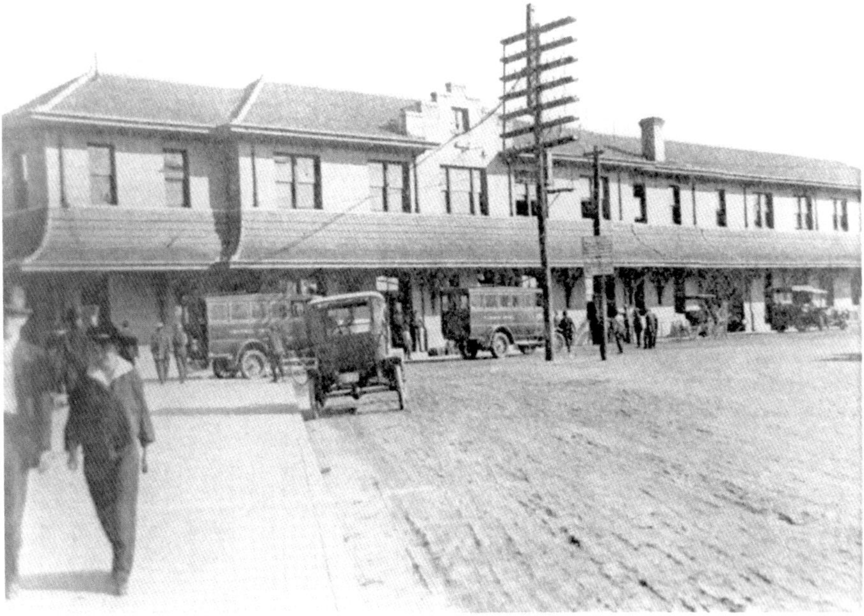

Old ACL passenger station, now a McLeod Regional Medical Center office building. *Courtesy of Wayne King.*

new train without responding, apparently having had enough reviews. (At least one published report puts the incident with the cadets at Mars Bluff, but it is more likely that it would have been at the Florence junction.)

The last station that Robert E. Lee visited here probably was at the corner of Church and Front Streets and the first was at Coit and Front. The ACL moved to the Day Street location about 1908.

A less welcome visitor six years before Lee's final visit was a detachment of Sherman's troops that came from near Cheraw to destroy the Florence railroad junction and free Union prisoners at the Florence Stockade. A superior Confederate force happened to be here, and after the Skirmish at Gamble's Hotel, the Union troops were chased back toward Darlington. The junction survived, and the prisoners already had been moved anyway.

Several presidents came through by train, but only William Howard Taft got off for a scheduled engagement here. Grover Cleveland came through while president in the nineteenth century, and he might have been the first. Herbert Hoover came through in January 1929 while president-elect, and the *Morning News* commented, "The president-elect did not as much as bestow a nod on Florence where a few years ago he was made the lion of a monster meeting."

A very big event at the Day Street Atlantic Coast Line station, now a McLeod Regional Medical Center office building, was when President Franklin D. Roosevelt stopped one night. There was great secrecy to prevent a crowd from developing, but, of course, there was a leak, and it seemed that half of the town turned out. The crowd pleaded until a shade was opened at his window and FDR waved to the cheering throng. They were not satisfied, so finally he came to the rear platform and made a few remarks.

The late Tommy Griffin liked to tell about being there when FDR came through, when he was a youngster working in the baggage room. Security was very tight, and armed soldiers were on the train shed and other places

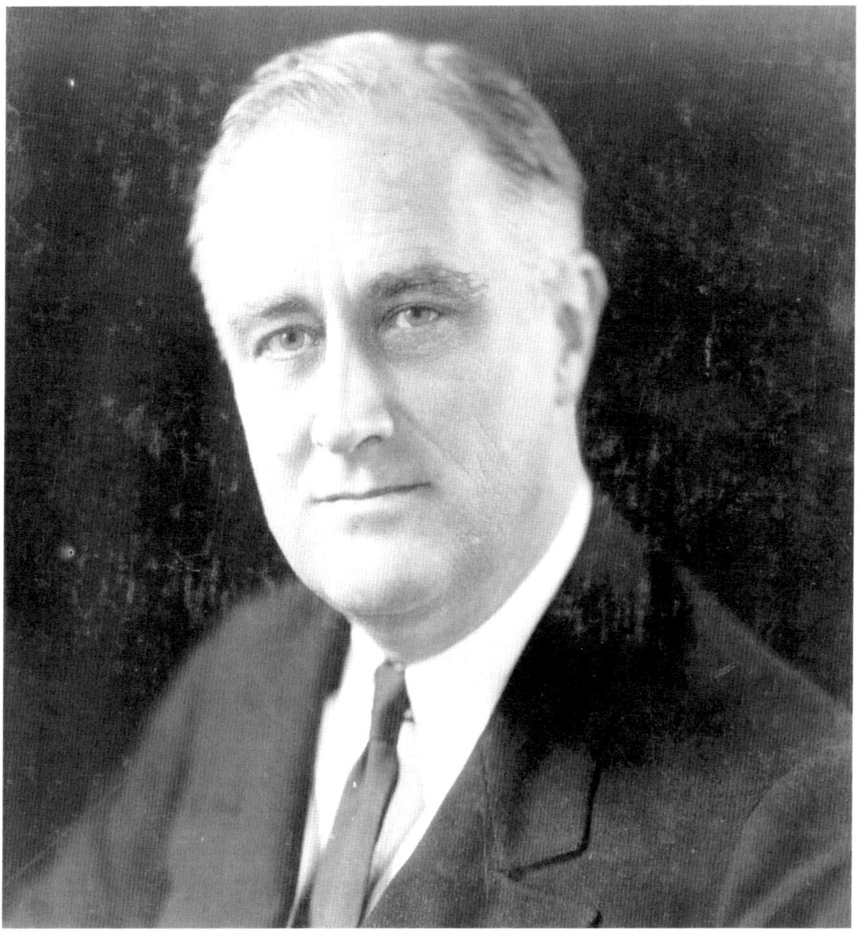

Franklin D. Roosevelt appeared at a Florence railroad station. *Courtesy of the Library of Congress.*

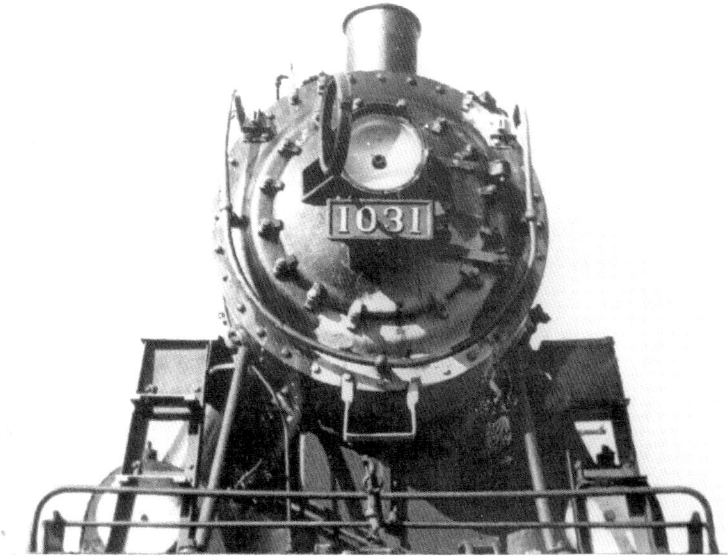

In 1959, the Atlantic Coast Line Railroad donated one of its last steam locomotives to the city of Florence. It was number 1031, a Baldwin 4-6-0, built in 1913. It was placed with a marker beside the tracks at Church and Baroody (then Front) Streets. A park-like setting was established, but later, when street alignments changed, it became less accessible and interest declined. Maintenance not being Florence's strong suit, the locomotive got little except for limited volunteer work and deteriorated badly. Finally, it was donated to a railroad museum in Spencer, North Carolina, where it has been treated better. *Courtesy of Wayne King.*

around the station, Griffin said. He also told of seeing many celebrities come through and particularly remembered handling Betty Grable's baggage and seeing Clark Gable in the station restaurant.

In the 1980s, there was another crowd down there when Vanna White and Pat Sajak came through on a special train promoting their *Wheel of Fortune* TV show. As she was from Ocean Drive Beach, Vanna probably had family on hand.

While people traveled through, the station traveled, too, from Hoffmeyer Road to Day Street with a couple of stops in between. The Seaboard Railroad also established a station at Darlington and Irby Streets in about 1915. The rails are gone, but the building remains and is part of Trinity Baptist Church.

Timmonsville Governor

Lieutenant Governor Charles A. Smith led the Senate across the Statehouse lobby on January 14, 1915, to a joint legislative session that was to elect a circuit judge. As he ascended to the Speaker's position in the House, he was told that he was needed in the governor's office after the joint session. Smith went and found, much to his surprise, that he was now governor. Governor Cole L. Blease had unexpectedly resigned five days before his term was to end. That was the strange beginning of the five-day term of the only Florence County resident to occupy the office of governor.

On personal stationery, Blease had written a one-sentence resignation, giving no reason. Both legislative houses broke into enthusiastic applause when they learned of Blease's departure and Smith's elevation. Blease was very controversial and disliked by much of the legislature.

"Well, I'll certainly have a long time to serve," Smith said to people who congratulated him.

Although Smith had quickly taken the oath from the chief justice, the legislature thought that there should be a more formal ceremony, and the next day, Smith retook the oath before a joint session and then went down the Statehouse steps to make a public speech. In that address, Smith suggested that the governor and comptroller general jointly propose a budget that could be amended or reduced but not increased by the legislature, which was unenthusiastic about that idea. He also urged a referendum on Prohibition. States that prohibited alcoholic beverages "have placed the moral and

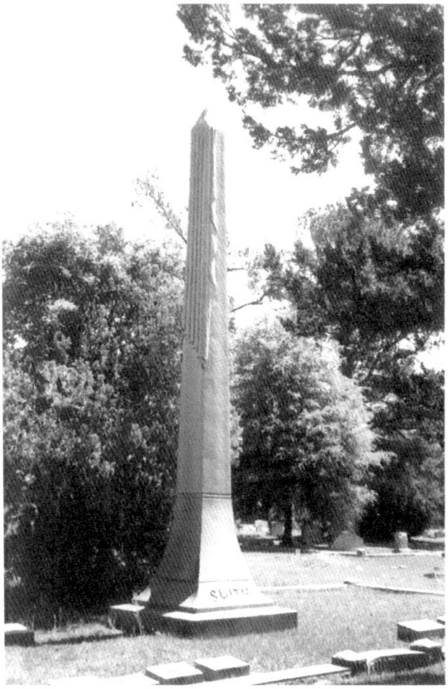

A monument in a Timmonsville cemetery marks the grave of short-term Governor Charles A. Smith.

temporal welfare of their citizens above the allurement of the unholy dollar," Smith told the crowd.

One of the first things Smith did as governor was appoint Blease notary public for Richland County.

Congratulations poured in for the new governor, most possibly arriving before his five days were over. A number were from Timmonsville. "I wish you could be governor always," read one hometown admirer's telegram. "Blease certainly did one good thing, anyway," read another.

Smith was born in 1861 in Hartford County, North Carolina, and was a graduate of Wake Forest College. Smith came to Timmonsville as a teacher and became a very successful businessman. He had an impressive record. In 1903, he was elected mayor of Timmonsville, serving until elected to the state House of Representatives in 1908. He was elected lieutenant governor in 1910 and 1912. He also served as president of the South Carolina Baptist Convention and vice-president of the Southern Baptist Convention and was president of the Furman College Board of Trustees.

The year after his five days as governor, Smith died at Johns Hopkins Hospital in Baltimore on April 1, 1916. He was buried in Byrd Cemetery in Timmonsville, where a spire marks his grave.

There was much speculation about the cause of Blease's abrupt resignation so late in his term. A *New York Times* article reported that Blease had boasted that Richard Irvine Manning would not succeed him. Manning had been elected and was to take office in five days, but giving Smith five days in the office made Blease correct: Manning did not succeed him.

Noah Would Have Felt at Home

The rainfall started before midnight, and at 4:00 p.m. on July 14, 1916, it still was going strong. There was high wind, too. Florence streets were impassable because of fallen trees, poles and wires, and bridges were washed away. A newspaper article reported, "The lovely shade trees on Coit and Irby, two of the loveliest residence streets in the state, are badly wrecked."

A tropical storm had come ashore at Charleston and caused havoc across the Southeast after an earlier storm from the west had soaked the area. Hurricanes Hazel and Hugo are well remembered, but the 1916 unnamed storm that brought Florence's greatest flooding is seldom remembered.

Henry H. Husbands signed an article from Florence that said the rainfall (14.25 inches) came over thirty-six hours. Road bridges on Jeffries, High Hill, Willow, Black and Beaver Dam Creeks and Polk Swamp were washed away. Rainfall at Effingham was 13.25 inches, and Kingstree recorded 31.5 inches during July.

Husbands feared that the Atlantic Coast Line Railroad trestle over Jeffries Creek just south of the city would be washed away, and it was estimated that two public bridges lost on Jeffries Creek would cost the county "upwards of $10,000" to replace. The two county bridges lost were at "Coles" and "Sycamore," probably where bridges now are on James Jones and South Cashua Drives. It was feared that the Lynches River road bridge would be lost. Replacement would cost $60,000.

A train crew arriving from Savannah reported no problems between Savannah and Charleston but difficulty between Mount Holly and Florence. It reached Florence four hours late and reported washouts above Kingstree.

An ACL work train from Florence was caught between washouts. The Florence railroad shops were shut down, and the railroad's water pumping station at Jeffries Creek was flooded under five feet of water.

Lake City had "unquestionably the worst storm ever witnessed by any living person here." Rainfall estimates were twelve to twenty-six inches, based on measuring levels in exposed cans. ACL tracks and the station there were flooded, and the *Williamsburg County Record* reported that "on Acline Avenue in front of the Rowell store, it was five feet deep." Boys played on makeshift rafts. Lake City stores were flooded, with twenty inches of water standing in some and goods damaged. Hundreds of chickens were drowned. Water rose so high that pigs swam over fences and escaped. All road bridges over Lynches Lake were washed out. There was no storm drainage system in Lake City at the time, but the experience convinced town officials that they needed one.

Of the seventy-five trains due in Florence on the worst day, only one arrived. Others were detoured. The ACL superintendent in Florence, E.B. Haire, said on July 17 that all lines were open except that from Lane to Florence. Trains from Charleston detoured through Orangeburg, Sumter and Darlington to Florence.

Telephones in Florence were out, and electric service was sporadic. Utility poles and lines were down all over the area.

A railroad worker on a tower near the ACL's Pee Dee River bridge reportedly had been ordered to stay at his station but said that "the tower is going, and I am too," as he jumped to safety. Seaboard Railroad bridges over Willow and Jeffries Creeks were reported washed out.

There was much concern in Florence over a small colony of Florence people at Pawleys Island who had not been heard from since the storm. Hartwell M. Ayer and a party set out to Pawleys to check on them and, caught by the flood, waded in waist-deep water to Seaboard tracks. Then, newspaper reports said, they walked to Mullins and finally made their way to Conway, planning to get a boat to Pawleys Island. The Florence colony was found safe and sound.

Downtown Florence, always difficult to drain, saw businesses and residences flooded. In the area north of the railroad yards, water stood two to five feet deep. "Every building in the city leaked as though they were sieves," a newspaper said.

"The various counties of the Pee Dee are going to be almost bankrupt," the *News and Courier* reported, because crops were nearly destroyed, and counties and towns were going to be saddled with huge repair bills for roads and bridges.

In addition to Florence's other problems, the roads and bridges that brought much business to the city's merchants were devastated. Stripped of revenues by damage, the city and county faced expensive repair bills.

Florence to Broadway to Hollywood

Florentines will have an opportunity of seeing one of their own girls before the footlights," the *Florence Evening Herald* declared in its issue of March 8, 1904. The "girl" was billed as Virginia Howell, a stage name that she adopted as a professional, but she was better known in Florence as Sophie Kuker. *Why Women Sin*, a touring play in which she was cast, was to be performed at the Opera House, which was part of the then new city hall. The 1904 newspaper article said that Miss Kuker, "one of the most popular and talented of the troupe," was from Florence and "has made a great success on the stage and whose praise is loudly sung wherever she appears."

Sophie Kuker decided to take a stab at professional acting after having success in local productions in Florence. There was amateur theatre in Florence nearly as long as the town existed. She came from a family that was interested in music and theatre, and after she left Florence, members of her close family were involved early with Florence theatre. Her parents were Mr. and Mrs. Theodore Kuker.

In *Why Women Sin*, she had an important role, newspaper articles of the period said, and the company was on a southern tour. It was reported that the schedule would take them to Danville, Virginia, and then to a couple of North Carolina stops before Florence on April 4, 1904. Miss Kuker was said to have played in nearly every state in the union, and after the play's tour of the South, she would have played in all but one of the—at the time—forty-five states.

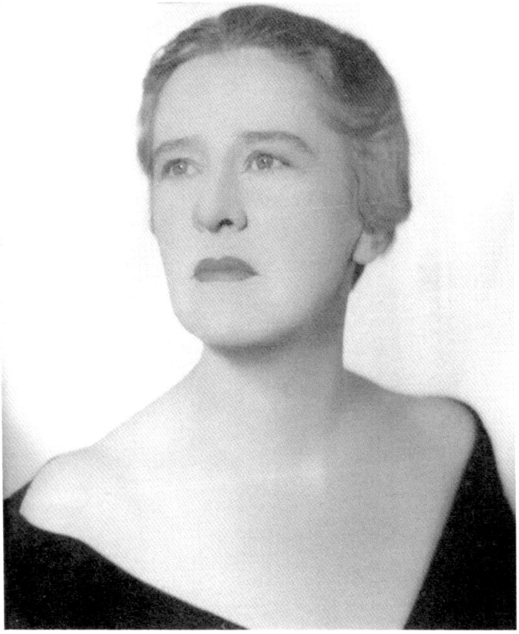

Sophie Kuker. *Courtesy of Pat King.*

"Florentines will turn out en masse to see Miss Kuker play, and from the notices which have greeted her efforts in the newspapers, no one will leave the play undelighted with her genius," it was predicted.

Perhaps her greatest achievement was in a production of *Ben Hur*, a great success in New York that was touring then. In that play, Pat King of Florence said, he was told that they had horses on stage that ran on treadmills. King, who is a great-nephew of Miss Kuker, said that when she landed her first part in New York, her name posed a problem, and they wanted a new name for her. He does not know why the name was a problem. She took Virginia, which was the name of her niece, he said, and Howell was the name of the director. Thereafter, she was billed as Virginia Howell.

She appeared with many famous stars and was in a play called *Hell's Bells*, which starred Humphrey Bogart and Shirley Booth. It was in that show that Bogart, carrying a racket across the stage, uttered the famous line, "Tennis, anyone?" That show in 1925 had 125 performances. Successful shows then did not have the very lengthy runs that they have now. Apparently her longest Broadway run was in the *Ziegfeld Follies of 1922*, which ran more than a year. Will Rogers was in that one.

"She had her greatest success on the stage in New York," King said. Later, she went to California to try the movies. "She got lots of small parts but never did the big things she hoped to do there," King said.

Internet Movie Database, which modestly bills itself as "the biggest, best, most award-winning movie site on the planet," lists twenty-nine movies in which she appeared, several uncredited.

"She and Jeanette MacDonald became good friends, and she was in a movie with MacDonald and Nelson Eddy," King said. While in

California, he added, Miss Kuker helped as Miss MacDonald prepared for her wedding.

Sophie was in *The Women*, which starred Joan Crawford, and she had a small part in *Little Women*, which starred Katherine Hepburn and Joan Bennett and was directed by George Cukor.

King said that the Kuker family lived in a house on the northeast corner of Palmetto and Coit Streets. As was often the case in the nineteenth century, the kitchen was separate from the house, and part of the kitchen structure still stands. According to her obituary in the *Morning News*, Sophie studied in Florence and in Belmont, Maryland, before striking out for a career in theatre.

King remembers one return to Florence by Miss Kuker, or Virginia Howell, as she was known then except in Florence. "She drove here from California," he said, "then drove from here to Chicago," where she was hoping her career would be rejuvenated. After that, "she would drop me a line, and I wrote to her," King said. A few years later, she broke a hip and went to Houston to be with her sister, Theo. She died there on January 1, 1942.

According to her obituary, her body arrived in Florence a day after her death and was taken to her nephew, Pat King's house. Besides her sister, Mrs. W.E. (Theo) Kendall, surviving was a brother, Didi Kuker, of Scranton, Pennsylvania. The funeral was held on January 3, 1942, at St. Anthony Catholic Church, with Father William A. Tobin officiating. Kuker was buried in the family plot at Mount Hope Cemetery.

Florence Little Theatre

There was amateur theatre in Florence in the nineteenth century. In old newspapers, mentions have been found of productions in the Gamble Hotel, the early village's most impressive building. Community theatre more formally existed starting with the Pinewood Players, who performed at the old Pinewood Club near Five Points soon after World War I. It is doubtful that those old hands could have imagined how their successors would have developed early in the twenty-first century. The Pinewood Players evolved into the Florence Little Theatre, and along the way, they performed in backyards, school auditoriums, borrowed storerooms and other places.

Soon after World War II—after having suspended production during the Great Depression and again during the war—the group reorganized and took the name Florence Little Theatre. They also got their first permanent home. It wasn't much, compared to where FLT is now, but it was a big step for the group. It was a small movie house that the army had built for airmen serving at the Florence Army Air Field during World War II. It was not equipped for live theatre. The stage was very small, and there were no dressing rooms, no room for storing or working on scenery and no wing space.

But there was a lot of talent in the organization, and their audience expanded. There were improvements. A small wing was added that gave a little room for scenery and for a degree of privacy in dressing rooms.

In the '50s, FLT decided to try Broadway musicals, although there was barely room to squeeze in a piano between the front row and the stage.

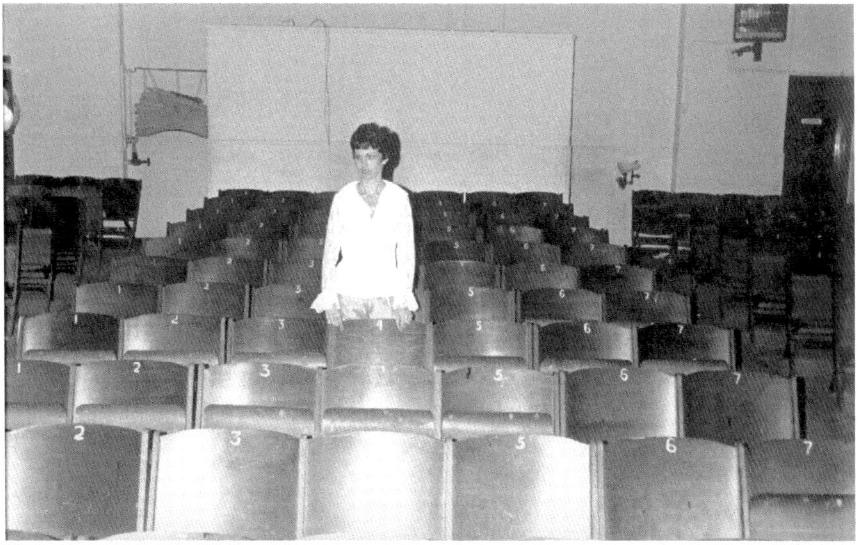

Patsy Stone inside FLT's first home at the Florence airport. *Courtesy of FLT.*

Pajama Game in 1958 was the first musical at the airport. Others followed, and audiences grew.

In the 1960s, FLT members decided that they must pursue their dream of a real theatre. They raised about $160,000 and had a lot donated on Cashua Drive. In November 1968, there was a grand opening for the next building. On Cashua there were real dressing rooms, a much bigger stage with good wing space, room to work on scenery and store it, twice as many seats and a real lobby and restrooms, in addition to a real parking lot. It had lighting capabilities undreamed of at the airport.

The grand opening was indeed grand, with tuxedoes and gowns and Governor Robert E. McNair leading the list of dignitaries who heaped praise on FLT for its accomplishments and on the community for supporting it.

The theatre hosted community meetings and special events of other organizations, and even housed St. Anthony Catholic Church while it was rebuilt after having burned down.

Musicals fit better in the Cashua house, and audiences grew as the theatre improved. It got special recognition when it received the Elizabeth O'Neil Verner Award, the state's highest award for contribution to the arts.

When FLT occupied its fine Cashua home in 1968, it would have been hard to imagine the theatre outgrowing it, but as the twenty-first century turned, it was realized that the space was no longer suitable. FLT members contemplated renovations and additions. Then came an offer from the

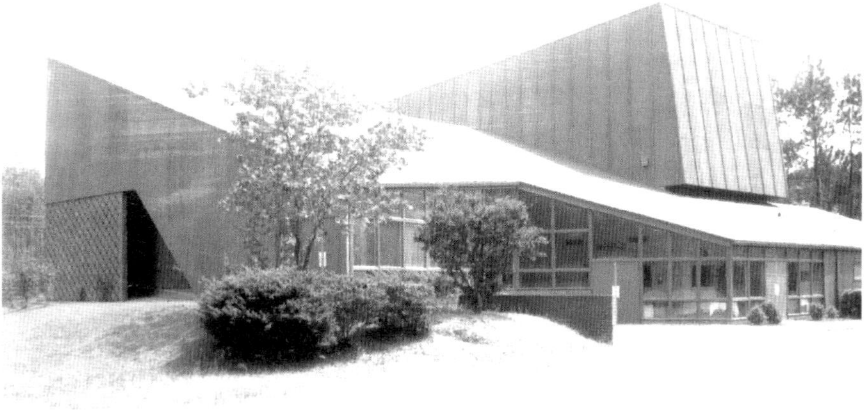

This Cashua Drive theatre was FLT's home until 2008. *Courtesy of FLT.*

Drs. Bruce and Lee Foundation to donate $10 million for a new theatre on South Dargan Street.

The city donated some property and McLeod Regional Medical Center an adjacent office building, and in September 2008, the first season opened on South Dargan Street. Spacious dressing rooms, scene shop and lobby were just some of the features of what must be one of the finest community theatre buildings in the country. It even has its own rehearsal hall, and theatre members do not now have to beg for rehearsal space while waiting for the preceding show to close.

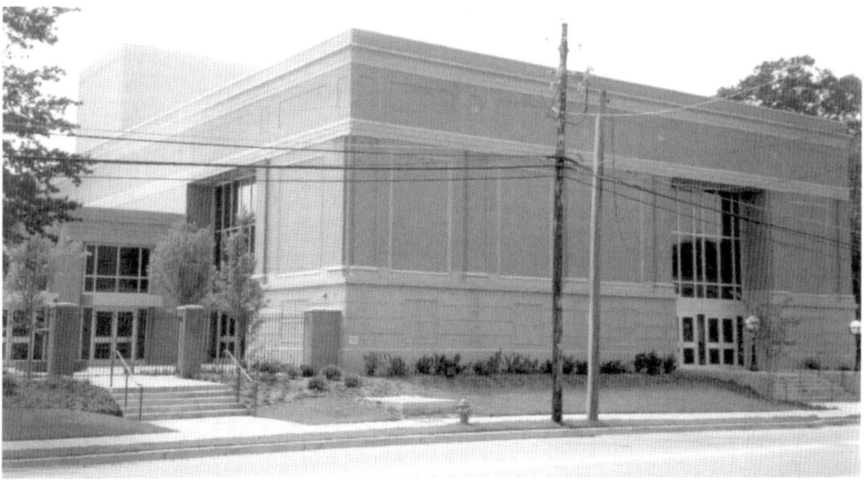

The Little Theatre's new $10 million home on South Dargan.

When the new theatre opened with another tux and gown event, it was next door to the splendid Drs. Bruce and Lee Foundation Florence County Library and a block from the Francis Marion University Performing Arts Hall, which was under construction.

Florence High's First Annual

Morning News column, April 21, 2002

Dedicated to former teachers…and many former students who…have patriotically joined…the great army that is fighting to 'make the world safe for democracy.'"

You probably recognize Woodrow Wilson's words at the end of that statement and would properly guess that it comes from the World War I period. It is the dedication of the 1918 *Florentine*, the first annual ever published by Florence High School seniors. I ran across it at the County Library recently, and for a first effort by a small-town high school, this annual looked like a pretty doggone good job to me. The book includes a picture of a school you would have to be a veteran Florentine to remember. It was on the 100 block of East Cheves Street, set on what is now part of the parking lot for the Department of Health and Environmental Control building. The school was razed about 1940 and replaced by two automobile dealerships.

In the 1970s, so-called "urban renewal" created Little Hiroshima in what had been the business district east of Dargan Street.

Browsing in the annual, which had a soft cover but otherwise was much like most other annuals you have seen, I ran across names from early in Florence public school history. The principal and Latin teacher of Florence High School was "Professor" George Briggs, who remained principal into the 1940s. Old-timers will recognize the names of the school board members, all white, of course, and all male: N.W. Hicks, chairman; J.W. Ivey; H.E.

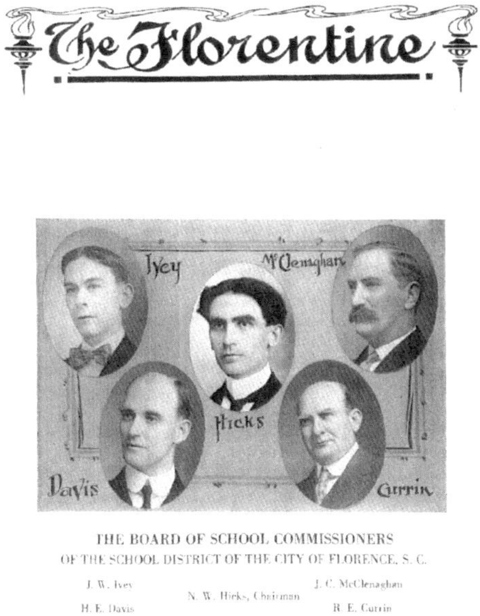

A page from the first FHS annual in 1918. *Courtesy of the Florence County Library.*

Davis; R.E. Currin; and J.C. McClenaghan, for whom the school was later renamed. W.L. Brooker was superintendent.

Among local teachers were Florence M. McKenzie, Marie Gregory and Margie Scarborough. Miss McKenzie later was principal of Circle School, which was renamed for her during the 1940s. Miss Gregory taught at the high school until the late 1940s. Miss Scarborough, I believe, was one of three Scarborough sisters who taught in Florence schools.

Briggs Elementary School was named for George Briggs, so among the board members and faculty were people for whom three Florence schools later were renamed: Briggs School, McKenzie School and McClenaghan High.

Listed in the freshman class was young Alice Brunson, who later taught high school English for many years. She was the sponsor of my class of 1950. Maybe there should have been a school named for her.

The year 1918 was a big one for the Florence school. The *Yellow Jacket*, the student newspaper, started during that school year. It boasted of FHS state football titles in 1916 and 1917 and a girls' basketball state championship in 1918.

The annual includes a brief history of Florence schools. It says that all of the city schools had been housed in that Cheves Street building until 1908. Before that two-story brick building opened in the mid-1890s, classes were held in several wooden buildings.

In 1908, all grades, it said, moved to the new Central School, now Poynor, but it was too crowded. The high school moved back to Cheves Street and "will be used until the modern building is erected." That happened in 1921, when the Florence (later McClenaghan) High building opened on South Dargan.

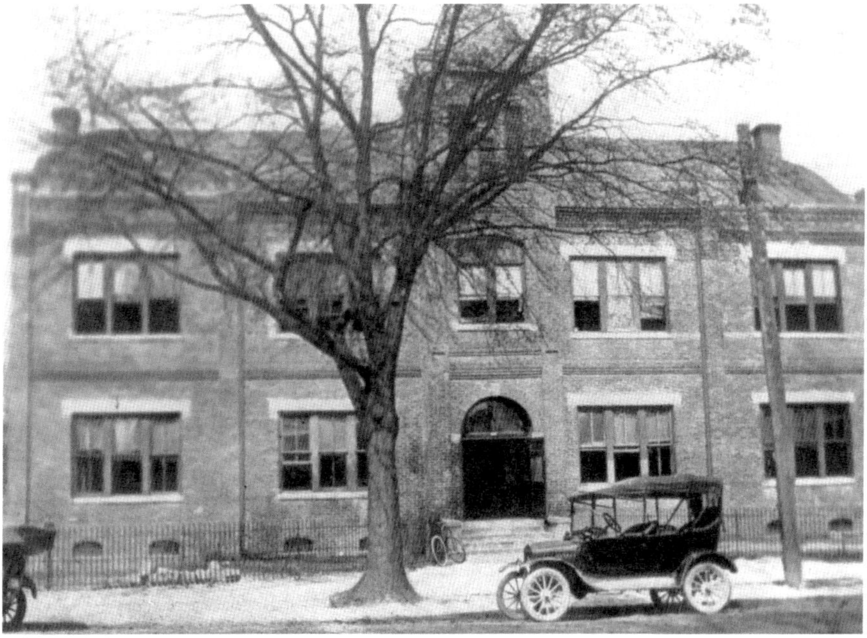

Florence High School was located in this building on Cheves Street in 1918. *Courtesy of Wayne King.*

It was an exciting time of vigorous growth in Florence. In 1910, there were 81 students in the high school. In 1918, there were 265. Total enrollment for all schools was 1,019 in 1910 and 2,786 in 1918. There were 17 teachers in white schools in 1910 and 40 in 1916. The schools were rigidly segregated at the time, and the annual makes no other mention of the "colored" schools.

I also learned that Park School, later Harllee, on East Pine Street was already there. Pictures portrayed Central (Poynor), Park (Harllee) and the Cheves Street school buildings. The annual states that the school had awarded state diplomas "for the last six years" and was accredited by the Southern Association.

The staff that produced the first *Florentine* included Eben Taylor, Franklin Morrison, Alston Wilcox Blount, Exum Lamar Lindsay, Margaret Howard, Catherine Lawton, Flora Barringer, James William Gee, Sadie Wells McEachin, Wilson S. McCall, Laurie Gorman, William Cooper and Maribel E. Waters.

The editors asked readers to "join them and with the Florence schools in the pardonable pride they have in the story the annual tells."

Folks, I did join them, and I am proud of that first FHS annual.

Fred Young's Most Famous Cow

Her full name was Sensation's Mikado Millie, but she apparently was best known as just Mikado Millie. She was a Jersey cow that had a prodigious production of milk and topped that by becoming the only Florence cow to have a U.S. cabinet officer visit her. Secretary of Commerce Herbert Hoover came to Florence in 1925, three years before he was elected president, and during that trip he had his picture snapped with people who were showing him around. Millie was in front of them in pictures when Hoover visited the Fred H. Young farm between Florence and Timmonsville.

Millie's fame was sensational enough that the *Middletown* (New York) *Daily Herald* carried a front-page story on her production. That paper reported that the two-year-old cow on Young's farm had set a world record in one year by producing 850.31 pounds of butterfat and 13,303 pounds of milk.

Hoover created considerable excitement by visiting Florence to make a much anticipated address to the Florence Chamber of Commerce. While in Florence, he concentrated on encouraging business activity, and the visit to the Young farm was part of that.

Excitement started in February 1925, when Senator E.D. Smith announced that Hoover would make a visit to Florence to speak at a chamber of commerce function. A local newspaper said that there would be an audience of about 250 "representative businessmen of the Pee Dee." In its "Did You Ever Stop to Think" column, in which it often expressed opinions about local happenings, the *Morning News* said that Hoover was "presidential timber." Hoover would, the paper said, "bring us a message of the good times ahead for all who will spend part of their time working instead of all the time grumbling." The appearance was set for March 23 as Hoover returned through Florence from a trip to Florida.

It was reported that Hoover had asked the chamber to circulate a questionnaire to find out what the audience would like for him to talk about. He wanted the results ten minutes before speaking. "Mr. Hoover carries his knowledge in his head, evidently," the paper commented. Afterward, it added that Hoover's was "the most perfect brain machine in the world." This comment is interesting, considering how people felt about Hoover *after* his presidency.

Among other things, Hoover said that Prohibition was paying off. He said that he was in Florence to see how a typical southern farming section was dealing with the day's economic difficulties. (The Great Depression is said to have arrived earlier in areas like the Pee Dee and stayed longer than in other sections.)

Hoover was a guest of Dr. F.H. McLeod during the visit, and he met community leaders at a pre-banquet luncheon. He urged businessmen and farmers to work together, but farmer Charlton Durant warned that Florence was not typical of this area, since "its biggest crop is the Atlantic Coast Line Railroad," Florence's biggest employer.

Visiting the Young dairy farm was a part of Hoover's educational tour, and the press reported that he would see Millie, "queen of Fred Young's herd" and the South's first world champion of any breed. A New York state newspaper that reported on Millie said that during the year she won the world championship, she produced $600 worth of milk while consuming $225 worth of feed. Also, Millie had produced her first calf, a bull for which Young had rejected an offer of $5,000, instead adding the bull to his herd. Millie was Fred Young's second Jersey Medal of Merit cow. Earlier, Belle de Sarah was South Carolina's first Medal of Merit winner.

The *Darlington News and Press* reported, "The good of Millie's ancestors is concentrated in her. The poor has been eliminated by avoiding it…Millie is just one of nature's steps to something higher and better."

Ed Young was an interested youngster of about five when Hoover visited. He got involved enough to wind up in some of the photographs. He recalled that his father tried to keep him out of the picture, but he got in anyway. "I just walked over and got in the picture," he said. Young remembered the excitement of Hoover's visit. "The press was here, and there was a lot

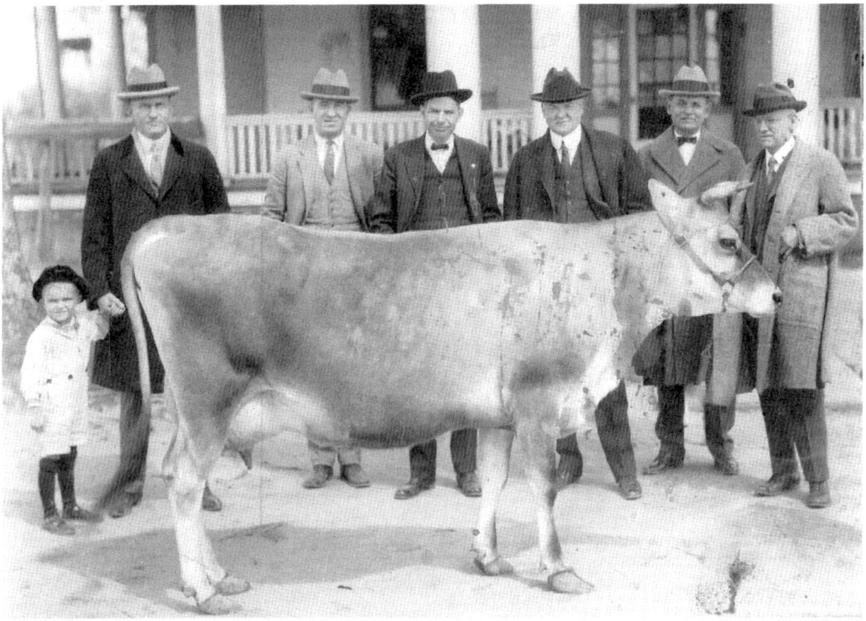

Behind Millie, from left, are five-year-old Ed Young, T.B. Young, W.J. Keegan, Fred Young, Herbert Hoover, D.W. Covington and Bright Williamson. *Courtesy of Ed Young.*

going on." Getting into the picture must have been a sign of things to come for the youngster. Decades later, Ed Young served in the state House of Representatives and later was elected to Congress.

There was at least one other highly productive cow that got the secretary's attention, but Millie remained the star of the show. (The Darlington County Historical Commission has at least one other picture from the visit, with Fred Young and Hoover the only people in the photograph but Millie still in front of them.)

Ed Young said that his father bought Millie from a breeder in Bishopville who had named her. He did not know the derivation. To get the two cows that he wanted, his father had to buy a third. That turned out to be Millie.

"Cotton had sold well in 1919," Ed Young said, but about then, farm experts who visited his father's farm spotted a boll weevil. His father knew what that meant for the future of cotton, so "he switched to dairy farming." The Young operation was a dairy farm for decades, but in 2009 it concentrates on beef cattle.

Millie had other calves, all bulls, but none of the bulls passed on Millie's ability to produce. Mikado Millie got newspaper attention in an ironic way during the 1970s. In a newspaper article, Herbert Jackson was said to have "tended to that bull [referring to Millie], as well as others on the Young farm." She also was called a "prize Guernsey bull."

This drew comments from readers, and Jackson, who had milked Millie three times daily, confirmed that she was indeed a cow, which did not make her as extraordinary as a bull producing such milk would have been.

A President Visits Florence

"This evening fair Florence will put forward her daintiest foot," *The State* newspaper reported on November 8, 1909, as the town prepared for a visit by the president of the United States. President William Howard Taft was wrapping up a thirteen-thousand-mile tour through the West and South during his first year as president. He visited Columbia the day before and then boarded a train for Florence.

The feature of the Florence visit was a banquet at the new Central School that, by 2009, was a little more than a century old and had been renamed Poynor School. When Taft arrived at Central, he first appeared before the building and spoke to a big crowd on the school grounds and on Dargan Street.

Decades later, an elderly woman recalled having, as a girl, been taken to the event by her father. She remembered a big crowd and excitement but recalled little detail. She did recall "a big fat man with one light bulb burning over him talking to the crowd." That sounds like Taft.

The auditorium was furnished with tables to seat four hundred. State and national colors and small pine trees decorated the room. At Taft's request, the event was informal, but one presidential staffer confessed to being dazzled by local women. The women, members of the Civic Improvement Society, had decorated the tables with roses, chrysanthemums and other flowers and national colors.

Girls in white with sashes of red, white and blue served dinner. "I am proud to see that Florence has those from whom such fair handmaids may be selected," the president diplomatically said.

The first items served were punch, salad and celery. One account said that what the menu lacked in "elaboration" was forgotten in the "soulfulness" of the fish stew. The feature was Pee Dee pine bark stew. Taft remarked that he had been served by chefs all over the country and in Europe and the White House but had had nothing before like Pee Dee pine bark stew. This was taken locally as a compliment.

The president spoke approvingly of cotton prices, strong at the time, and said that this promised future prosperity. Boll weevils were yet to appear.

Taft echoed his predecessor, Theodore Roosevelt, on attacking monopolies. He said that economic growth should be on a basis of legality, integrity and morality. The country, he predicted, was beginning a great era of prosperity. He thought that Florence would also enjoy prosperity.

He expressed delight at "an intelligent audience like this" and stated that, despite accents, Americans were basically alike. Sectional differences had been ironed out, he said, adding that the warmth of his welcome indicated that Civil War bitterness was gone.

After dinner, cigars and coffee were provided, and a loving cup was presented to Taft by U.S. senator E.D. (Cotton Ed) Smith on behalf of the Order of Railway Conductors, Tillyaw Division of Florence. The president promised that the cup would be treasured.

"Goodbye, my old Scotch friend," Taft said to John McSween of Timmonsville as he shook McSween's hand vigorously. Then he left the hall, walked downstairs and went to his auto. He departed on a late train headed for Washington, apparently facing a few more stops.

"Fair Florence" had put on quite a welcome for Taft, the only sitting president to visit for a scheduled event. Other presidents have traveled through on trains and sometimes briefly spoke with people at the Atlantic Coast Line station.

On the president's arrival, members of the local militia unit formed an honor guard as Taft's party went to their vehicle, which joined a thirty-car procession. A "long avenue of people," news reports said, waited to see the president pass. They cheered and waved hats, and there was "special illumination." It was his third stop in South Carolina, and Senator Smith said that the Florence crowd was Taft's largest in the state. He had promised Taft that would be the case and was happy that his prophecy had proved correct.

Besides the street decorations, Taft also passed stores on downtown streets that had special decoration, and the Gem Theater offered five free passes that day for the militia honor guard, not specifying which five got the tickets. Banks and stores closed early.

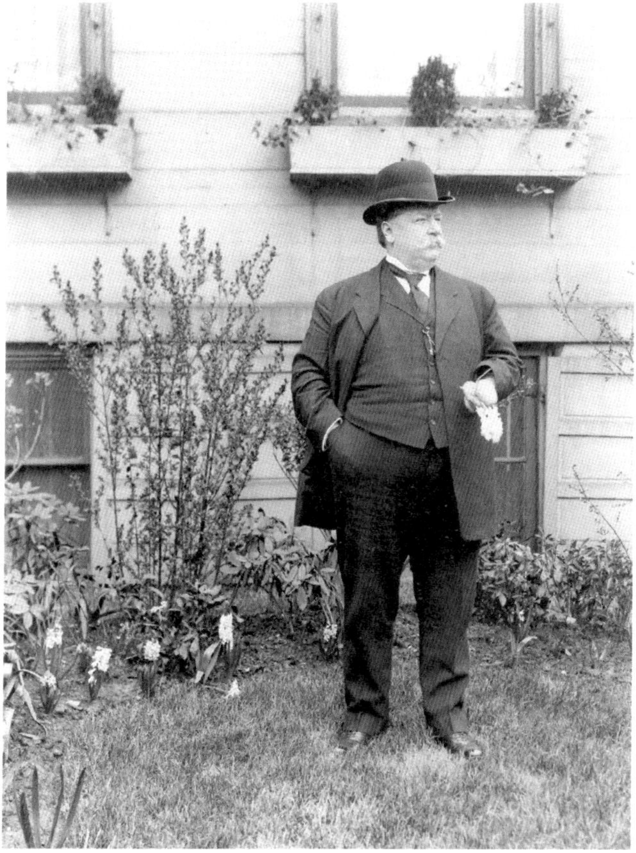

William Howard Taft. *Courtesy of the Library of Congress.*

The crowd was enlarged by an ACL offer of special low prices into Florence, giving area people a chance to see the president. On the way to Florence from Columbia, Taft spoke to a crowd at the Sumter train station.

After the excitement, the honor guard marched to the baseball park to camp overnight.

Dr. N.W. Hicks was chief marshal of the parade, and W.R. Barringer and Louis H. Meares were in charge of the welcoming functions. A big dance was held that night, but it is unclear whether Taft attended. The First Artillery Band provided music.

"Florence was gaily attired," one news report said, and "Florence as usual did itself and its state proud," a Columbia newspaper observed.

It probably was the biggest thing in Florence since three railroads in the 1850s created a junction around which the city developed—with the possible exception of an 1865 raid by a detachment of Sherman's army that was turned back.

Florence was a vigorous town with a population of 3,395 (1900 census) and would have 7,657 by 1910. It had become a county seat about twenty years earlier. Besides being a railroad center, it was also becoming the shopping center for eastern South Carolina.

Taft's visit coincided with a Pee Dee Convention, a gathering of area leaders to talk about economic plans. A hot topic was the possibility of a new railroad connection from the mountain coalfields to Charleston, increasing rail traffic through Florence.

PEE DEE PINE BARK STEW RECIPE

The secret, locals said, of Pee Dee pine bark stew, of which they were so proud, was its being cooked over a very slow fire of pine bark or dead tree limbs. The stew for Taft's night was cooked on the grounds in large wash pots said to be of an antebellum type. (It's safe to guess that the "bellum" referred to was the Civil War.)

The fish reportedly were caught with hook and line in the Little Pee Dee and Lumber Rivers and were the "finest variety of bream, red bellies and speckled trout."

The recipe, as reported in the *News and Courier*:

> *The fish first were thoroughly cleaned and salted.*
> *Bacon was put in and fried, the grease left in the pot.*
> *Tomatoes, tomato sauce, Cayenne pepper, Worcester sauce and onions were boiled for a half-hour.*
> *Then the fish were put into the pot and boiled for 35 minutes.*
> *It was taken off, cooled for a few minutes and served with pure South Carolina rice.*
> *Enough water was added to make a simple soup. (This was considered a feature of the stew.)*
>
> *C.L. Boinest was in charge of all this with Henry H. Rose as first assistant, Sheriff Thomas F. Burch second assistant and Morton Muldrow third assistant.*

Tornado Sweeps Across County

Witnesses said that a great black cloud covered the sky, obscuring the view of an approaching whirlwind. With poor visibility, when the whirlwind appeared, it was so close that there was little time to find cover. Funnel winds were estimated at more than two hundred miles per hour, and the funnel seemed to move at unusually high speed.

On April 30, 1924, a great storm swept across the state. It spawned a tornado known by names including Horrell Hill Tornado, for a Richland County community where a school was destroyed, and Aiken-Pamplico Tornado, which pretty much described its route.

Seventeen were reported dead in Florence County, and neighboring Darlington, Sumter and Lee Counties also had fatalities reported.

Some descriptions of incidents are chilling. One woman was said to have been thrown 150 yards across a field and killed. Furniture and boards from houses were carried a half-mile or more. A book from the Horrell Hill School, which was destroyed by the storm, was found in Florence County, eighty miles away. A Timmonsville-area woman whose house was destroyed was found dead about 100 yards away with her daughter and daughter-in-law nearby, critically injured. A man had a huge splinter from a shattered board driven through his body. He died. A woman died when she was impaled by a flying board. A five-week-old child reportedly was carried 100 yards on a mattress, where his mother found him "fully awake and unhurt." A boy was blown into a rye patch, shaken but not badly hurt. A woman was "picked from the road and hurled into oblivion." It was believed that five members of one family died, news reports said.

Apparently, many farm men escaped injury because they were transplanting tobacco and were relatively safe from flying debris from houses and barns. Mothers frantically sought children from whom they had been separated, "not minding their own wounds," the *Morning News* reported.

Four people, three of them children, died in Florence hospitals, and the number of injured threatened to overwhelm facilities and equipment. "There are doubtless others, particularly among the Negroes, unreported as yet," a news account said. Besides the county injured, several from Lamar in Darlington County were at Florence hospitals.

"Florence escaped the tornado," the *Morning News* reported. "There was not even a gale here, although for a few moments in the middle of the day there fell a heavy rain."

It came from the northwest through Sardis, passed near Effingham and lifted near Pamplico. "It left utter destruction in its wake," a news report said. Hundreds were reported homeless, with an estimated "two-

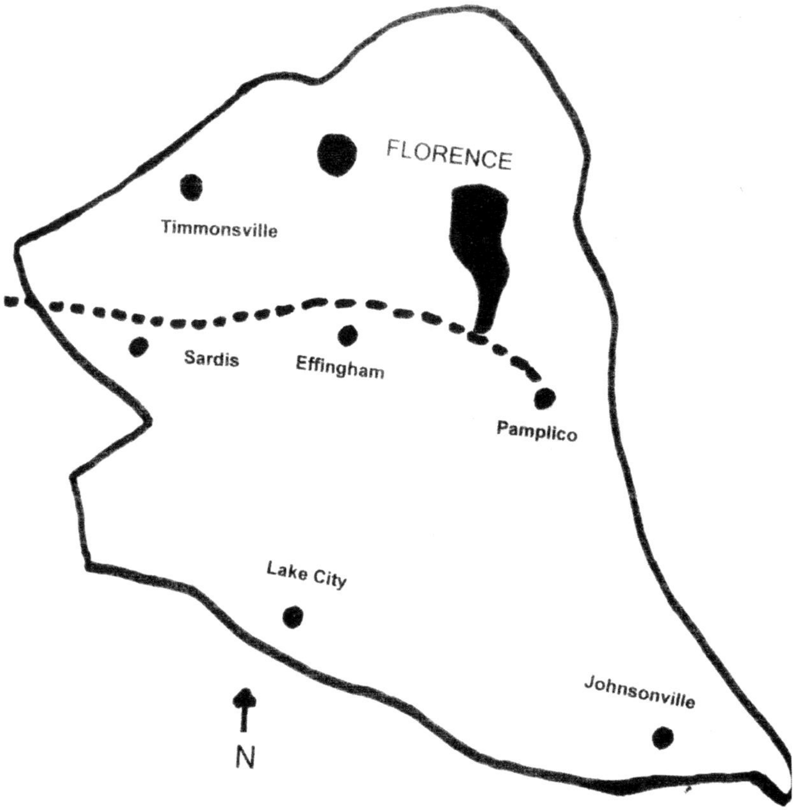

This map shows the route of the 1924 tornado across Florence County.

score" homes destroyed and many others greatly damaged. Countless barns and other outbuildings were destroyed along the thirty-mile route. Destruction was so complete that sometimes not even bricks from chimneys were found.

Crops were blown over. Livestock were panicked and often freed from pens. Cattle apparently were particularly hard hit, with many killed. It was said that a cow was lifted from a field and dropped into a barnyard, where she was found calmly enjoying some corn.

The county poor farm at Effingham was hit, though not severely damaged, but at Pamplico the Dargan Lumber Co. had a wing destroyed and its veneer plant damaged.

At the first home hit in Florence County, the house was badly damaged, a barn destroyed and three mules killed. A large neighboring home was destroyed but none of the fifteen people there were hurt badly.

The *Daily Times* reported that a man was hurled from his home but not badly hurt. He later found his pants hanging from a tree a half-mile away with money still in the pockets.

The afflicted area's neighbors were not indifferent. Florence mayor W.M. Waters issued a proclamation that called for people to "come to the aid of these unfortunate victims." Florence County pledged $1,000 for a relief fund, the Red Cross $1,000, the city $250 and the chamber of commerce $100. Waters appointed a committee to coordinate relief efforts, consisting of B.C. Chandler, chairman; J.C. Long; J.F. Stackley; H.B. McCall; and W.H. McElveen. Relief funds totaled more than $2,500.

Signs of the times were that the Ku Klux Klan donated $100 and promised more if needed, and a newspaper, citing the need of farmers, suggested "loan your negro and a mule," with a lowercase "n" on Negro, as was the custom then.

The American Legion promised two days of labor on the part of its membership to help fix the devastated area. Florence County also had a relief committee, composed of J.E. Baskin and M.H. Purvis of Timmonsville; B.C. Thomas and H.B. McCall of Elim; Stackley and Long of Florence; Joe M. Eaddy, G.B. Bowen and B. McElveen of Lake City; and W.H. McElveen of Sardis.

There was much interest on the part of outsiders, and that became part of the problem. An estimated twenty-five thousand people came to view the damage, "awed by the calamity of it all." A newspaper observed that "it must have made them think, because the driving was orderly, not one automobile accident being reported." Many visitors made donations to the relief fund, but it was also said that admission should have been charged because there was additional damage to crops by the "trampling thousands."

The tornado traveled 135 miles between Aiken County and the Pamplico area, where it lifted and was said to be headed toward Horry County. There were finally 67 counted dead and 678 injured in South Carolina on a day when there were outbreaks over the Southeast. In all, reports for the entire region set the death toll at 110 and 1,133 injuries.

One Fine City Block

Morning News column, July 8, 1973

They closed the doors of the P&M Café a week ago. Paul Economy had said that the business would close soon to make way for urban renewal, but it was a shock to learn on a Saturday afternoon that the day had come when the old place would close after seventy years.

Many longtime customers made one last visit to the restaurant, and they were rewarded with a few nostalgic moments, champagne on the house and what seemed like better-than-usual steaks. Among those who have been going there for years, tales were swapped about the people who used to work there and regular customers of years ago, of celebrities who were there when the block's old hotels flourished and other celebrated P&M incidents. Like the time the guy went too far demonstrating how this here tear gas canister works. He cleared the place and gave us a classic story.

The top story was about the recent robbery, when gunmen appeared in the café and took money and valuables from the business and the customers. The robbery was merely dramatic evidence of how things have changed on the block while the P&M went on.

Those of us who can remember the late '30s, the World War II period and the 100 block of East Evans Street remember it as the liveliest block in town. This may surprise you, but that block gave Florence much more of a big-town atmosphere than it has now. It never stopped. The old Hotel Florence and Sanborn Hotel stood across the street from each other, and they represented

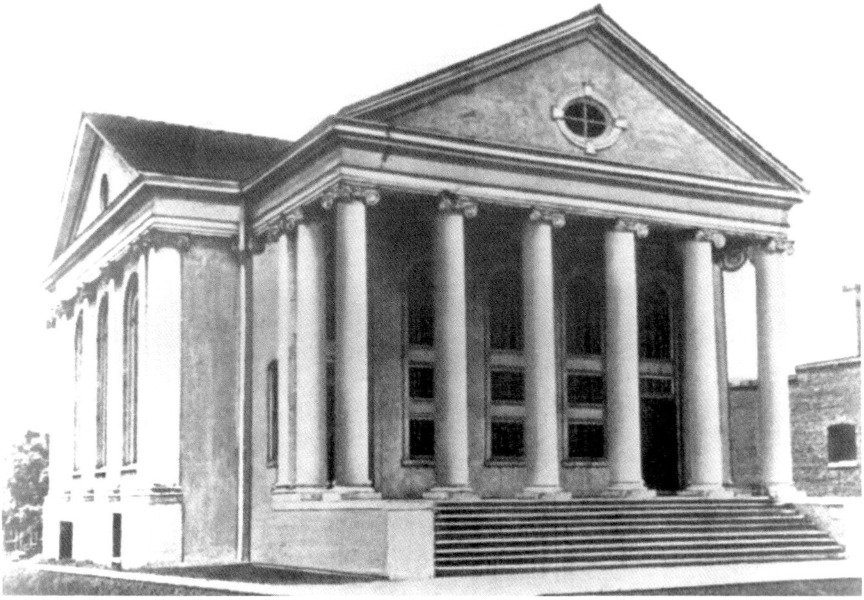

First Presbyterian Church was on East Evans until the early 1950s. *Courtesy of Wayne King.*

most of the accommodations in the state's most important railroad junction town when most long-distance travel was by train. Those hotels housed some of the best-known people in America as well as traveling salesmen, some of the Harold Hill type who could have stepped right out of *The Music Man*.

The *Morning News* was on that block. So was Western Union, and those were sources of activity around the clock. The Smoke Shop was in a building with a wooden floor and a little passageway that led directly into the lobby of the Hotel Florence. You could buy a newspaper there from all of the major cities on the East Coast. You cannot even buy a New York or Washington paper in town now.

There was a poolroom, a bowling alley for a while and the old Postal Telegraph, which challenged Western Union and was housed across the street from its competitor.

Radio station WOLS, the first broadcasting station in the eastern part of the state, started in a small suite of rooms on the ground floor of the Sanborn Hotel. A door opened under a sign saying WOLS, and I got at least one tour of the place before it moved to South Dargan Street. Russ Holt, a WOLS sports announcer, impressed me much more than Curt Gowdy, now famous on TV.

Every fortyish native of Florence must at some time have gone on a hot late summer day to the Hoffmeyer Brothers school supply and bookstore to

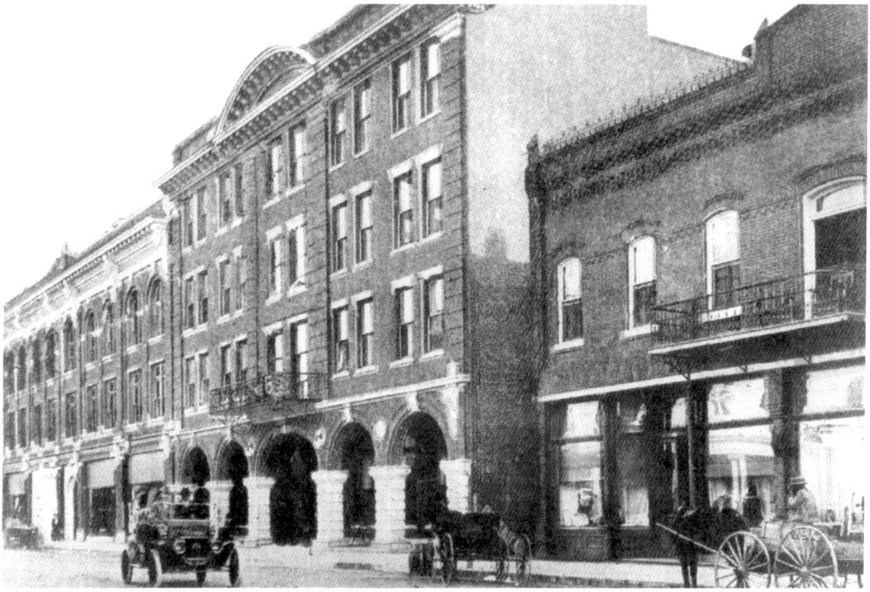

Hotel Florence was one of the main buildings on the 100 block of East Evans Street.

get ready for the school year. It was also a block where a large number of people lived. The Hoffmeyer brothers had an apartment over their store, and some upper floors along the block were apartments and lodging rooms. The old Williamson building where the *Morning News* once occupied a storefront was once a long, three-story building. What is left of it is one floor now.

Before network broadcasts were available, a championship boxing match meant big doings on East Evans. A big crowd would gather in the street in front of the *Morning News* at fight time, and a strong-lunged speaker such as Colonel Frank Barnwell would read round-by-round accounts of the fight direct from the Associated Press teletype.

They were delivered with a flourish, and the crowd would react to the news as if they were on hand for the fight. Between rounds, many in the crowd would duck into the alley beside the Sanborn for a quick drink. That alley never heard of Prohibition. It was also said that you could place a wager on the fight in that crowd.

City officials never dreamed of running a parade in those days without going through the block, even if the railroad tracks could complicate matters. It has been years now since one went through there.

If you ever forgot the importance of the railroads in those days, you got practical reminders every few minutes when another train came through and, if the wind was right, filled the block with thick, black coal smoke.

Diesels relieved that part of town of a lot of soot, but a lot of excitement, too. There was a railroad tower at the crossing where a switchman cleared traffic into the yards. I got tours of that, too.

Many evenings the boys who worked late at the *Morning News* watched Hotel Florence windows from the back lot and made book on which room would be worked first by the pros from the city's famous old red-light district.

Games of chance were also plentiful in hotel rooms, and there were a couple of places where you could place any kind of bet you had on your mind. The police miraculously overlooked a couple of ball score tickers and scoreboards not too well concealed on the block. In those days, the police were less concerned with imposing one's moral standards on another than they were with public safety.

Then there was the State Theatre. It was just across the tracks and was the one that showed the "adults-only" movies. I well remember several occasions when my parents thought I was at a cowboy show at the Carolina. I stood on tiptoes to shove my quarter through and receive my ticket just under the sign that said "Nobody Under 18 Admitted." Usually at those State adults-only movies you got to see some underwear, but there was one show

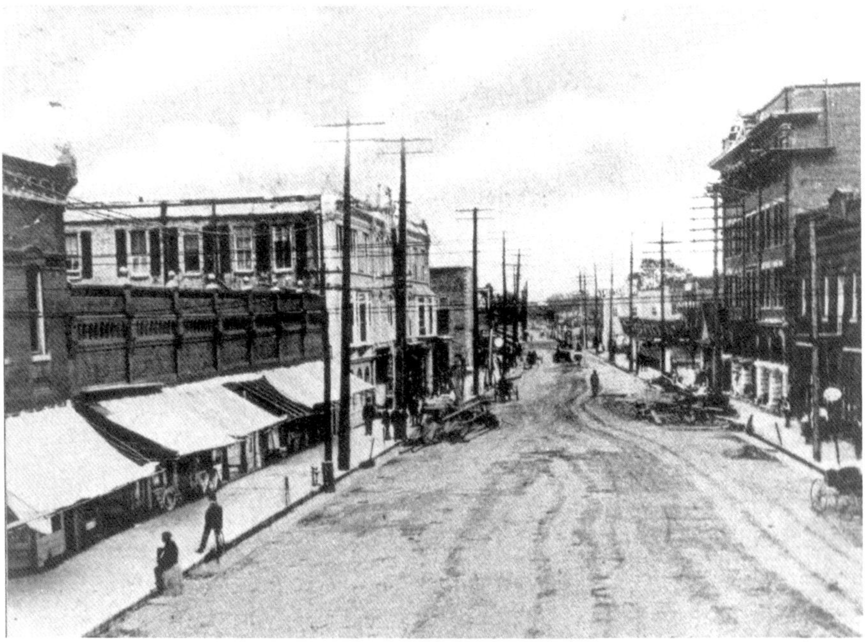

View down the 100 block of East Evans early in the twentieth century.

named *Marijuana*. A pale, thin fellow with a moustache and what looked like a doctor's white coat and a terminal case of tuberculosis appeared at the beginning of the film with a discussion of the evils of drugs, establishing redeeming social value before Earl Warren was even a district attorney in California. Anyway, we got a glimpse of breasts at one stage when the film showed a wild party at which teenagers played strip poker while under the influence of pot. It was the talk of the boys' basement at Poynor Junior High for weeks. Nowadays, it would be rated PG.

It was not all worldly. The parking lot across from the P&M was the site of the old First Presbyterian Church before it moved to its present site. It was an imposing old building set back behind a small yard between downtown business buildings. The church, sadly, was among the first of the block's institutions to go.

The P&M itself was much different at the end. There once was a counter to the left where many were served and a few booths on a black-and-white tile floor. When it closed, the counter was gone, the floor was carpeted and there were plusher booths.

The Salvation Army kept a high profile from its headquarters just across the tracks, and their band and street corner services were great on Saturday nights. It is said they were joined a few times during those services by a young Fuller Brush salesman named Billy Graham. Yep, that Billy Graham.

James Jones started his magnificent one-man crusade against polio on the block. He soon became renowned as "March of Dimes" Jones and won unusual community respect for a black man during that heavily segregated period.

On the block, the hotels are gone, the *Morning News* and WOLS are long gone. The church, car dealers, bakery and baseball tickers are gone. Florence is bigger and more spread out, but there is no place with the twenty-four-hour concentration of activity that used to be East Evans Street and that Damon Runyon–type style that a big-town atmosphere creates.

I never went to the P&M in recent years that I didn't think about watching that block as a kid and how much the town has lost with its passing. Now everything is scattered, and such an accumulation of activity in such a small area is not now possible in a town the size of Florence. East Evans just doesn't allow enough acres for those Detroit devils. I don't know what ever made me think Henry Ford was one of the good guys.

2009 Update: The P&M Cafe was not the last place on that block to shut down. Everything closed. What business decisions did not take down, urban renewal did, and the block was turned into a wasteland. Buildings have gone

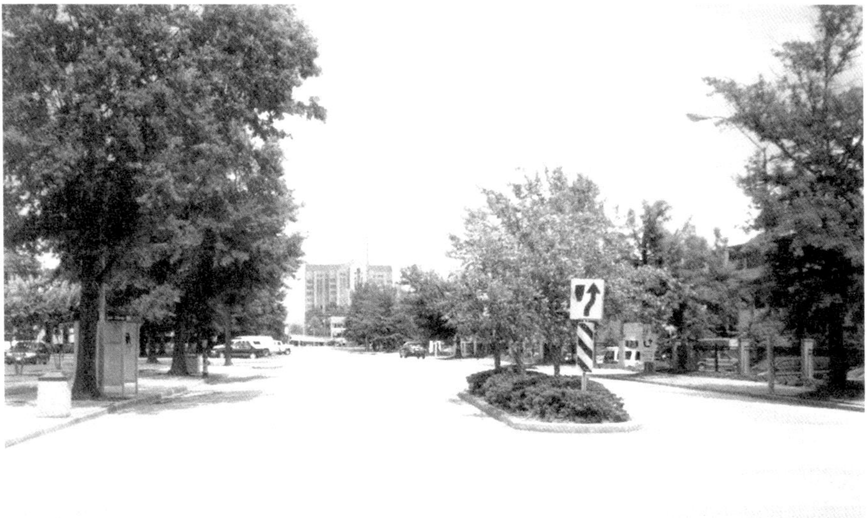

View down the 100 block of East Evans Street in 2009.

up on some of the cleared property, but now there is not a front entrance on the 100 block of East Evans. On the south side, two state-run medically related buildings front on Cheves Street and have their backs to Evans. On the north side, a wing of the Business and Technology Center that fronts on Baroody Street has side doors opening onto Evans. A ride through the block is saddening to veteran Florentines.

Sousa's Band Plays Florence High

Imagine being a high school band director and finding yourself conducting John Philip Sousa's famous band. That's what happened to Guy Hutchins, band director at Florence High School, in 1930. (It was about fifteen years before the school's name changed to McClenaghan High.) This is a complicated story that includes tennis, contract negotiations, Armistice Day observances and a vacant spot on Sousa's 1930 tour schedule.

Dr. Julian Price and Dr. Walter R. Mead learned that Sousa had concerts scheduled in Columbia and Charleston with room between for a date in a conveniently located city. Florence met that test, they figured, and they also wanted some public tennis courts in Florence. At the time, St. John's Episcopal Church had a court, and there was one at a residence. Those were the only tennis courts in town. St. John's was pretty generous about letting people use its court, but then, Price said years later, it was not much of a court.

If they could arrange a Sousa date in Florence, they might make enough money to build a public tennis court or two. They found that Sousa wanted $10,000 to appear, but they did not have access to $10,000. Dollars of 1930 were much more powerful than twenty-first-century dollars. They proposed splitting gate receipts without a guarantee. The March King agreed. He was to get 90 percent and Price and Mead's project would get 10 percent. It was billed as a farewell tour for the seventy-six-year-old Sousa, who died about two years later.

Sousa and his band played two concerts, and Price recalled that the audience was "a fair crowd, not too big." The *Morning News* called it "disappointing." However, it was enthusiastically received by the audience, the newspaper added.

The selections might have been a little surprising for people expecting Sousa marches. One was a suite that the conductor called "The Three S's," including pieces by Strauss, Sullivan and Sousa. "Mars and Venus," the Sousa part of the suite, was one of only two of his creations on the program. Included were works by Berlioz, Mulder, Wagner, Kreisler, Guion and others. The program was described as being "of a most artistic nature."

"Both audiences went wild," an unsigned review said. They "voiced their delight by demanding encores," and Sousa obliged them. Possibly the most enthusiasm was for soprano Marjorie King's performance of "Dixie." They were eighty years closer to the Civil War then.

More of Sousa's works were among the encores. One can imagine how the audience reacted when they heard "The Washington Post March" and

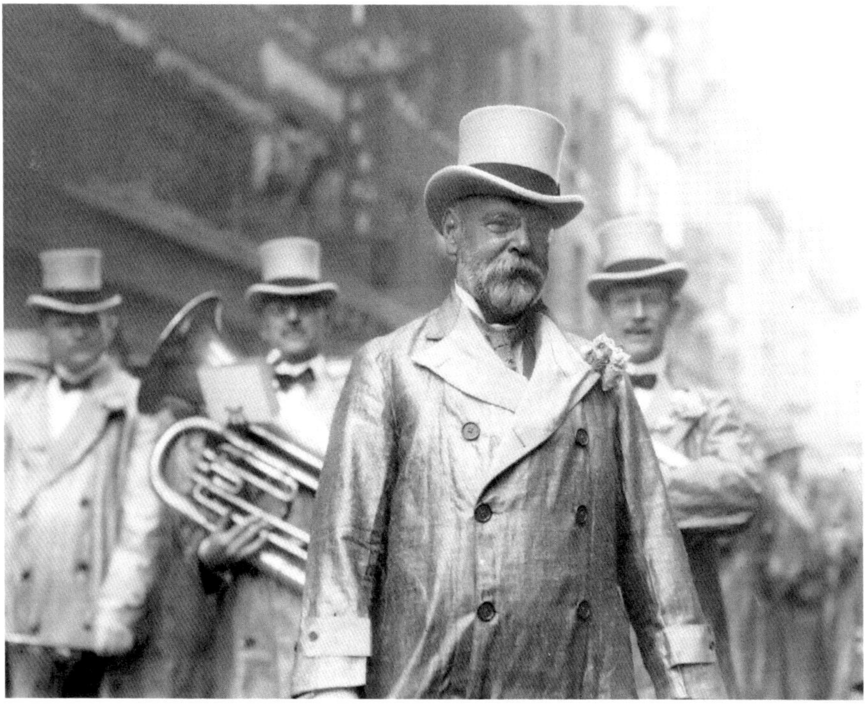

John Philip Sousa. *Courtesy of the Library of Congress.*

especially "Stars and Stripes Forever," conducted by the composer himself. "They almost made the walls fall down," Price said. The review enthused that Sousa was the "incomparable bandmaster who has played for kings and queens of many countries and whose compositions have been accepted everywhere as classics."

If Sousa was disappointed in the turnout, it did not affect his public relations. At one point, he delighted the crowd by inviting Hutchins to lead his band for a number. Earlier in the day, Sousa had conducted Hutchins's high school band in a performance for students.

He also attended a joint meeting of the Rotary, Kiwanis and Lions Clubs for Armistice Day, which marked the end of World War I and now is celebrated as Veterans Day. Sousa made the main address for that occasion. Editor Mason C. Brunson introduced Sousa while Price served as master of ceremonies.

While serious about the patriotic celebration, Sousa injected a little humor with his address, titled "How I Won the War." He joked that when the Kaiser learned that Sousa had shaved his famous beard and was coming, he was so frightened that he requested an armistice.

It was a big day for Price, who was responsible for escorting Sousa around town. "He was a very nice fellow," Price said, and spending time with him was really enjoyable. He learned that Sousa did not much like jazz and disliked radio, although he did conduct a few times on that medium. Television was in the future.

Price was a little bothered by the turnout, particularly because he felt there might have been more people from Hartsville than Florence. He figured that might have been because of the presence of Coker College there. It was forty years or so before the founding of Florence's Francis Marion University. He asked Sousa how to build interest in music, and the bandmaster said, "Start with the children."

A couple of then young Florentines were outside when the concerts took place. Decades later, Brooks McCall told of getting Sousa's autograph. He was proud and kept it in a desk in a barn. "A bunch of kids got in and tore everything up," including the Sousa autograph.

McCall also told of being at his aunt's house across Dargan Street from the school when Will Rogers made an appearance. He could not afford a ticket and did not see Rogers, but he soaked up the excitement.

Harvard E. Dudley was a youngster who later had a military career that included a tour on President Harry Truman's White House staff. Decades after Sousa's Florence visit, Dudley told about being unable to buy a ticket but slipping up outside stairs to the auditorium's stage doors and listening.

SOUSA
AND HIS
BAND

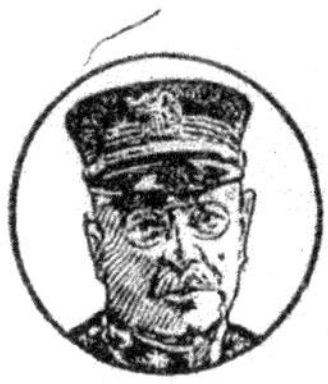

PROGRAM

Florence High School Auditorium

November 10, 1930

AUSPICES

FLORENCE ATHLETIC ASSOCIATION

The cover of the program for the famous band's performances in Florence. *Courtesy of Wayne King.*

Under the deal of Sousa getting 90 percent of the proceeds and the tennis project 10 percent, the gate was about $8,000. Sousa got $7,200 and the tennis project's payoff was about $800, which was considerably more in 1930 than it would be in the twenty-first century. The city gave Price and Mead space at Timrod Park to build two tennis courts. They are still there, rebuilt and joined by additional courts. The Atlantic Coast Line Railroad gave them cinders to serve as a base, and a property owner gave clay from a borrow pit. The phone company donated poles to erect a high fence. The $800 went for the fence and other equipment for the courts. The project was done thriftily and made tennis much more available in Florence.

Drs. Price and Mead got great satisfaction out of their success, but it is doubtful that anybody enjoyed the experience more than Guy Hutchins, the high school band director who led Sousa's band.

There is evidence that the 1930 appearance may not have been Sousa's first in Florence. A Kingstree paper of January 23, 1908, reported that "quite a party of [Lake City] people went up to Florence Friday to hear Sousa's band." They were "delighted, not to say amazed" at the performance, the item said, and "it was a rare opportunity to hear one of the most famous bands on earth—in fact, many critics give this band the very first place."

Film Looks at 1930s Florence

Morning News column, December 12, 1979

The narrator said, "This is the police chief. The name, I believe, is McErvin." "McIver! McIver!" shouted a good part of the crowd.

At another point, the old Fairfield Dairies was shown and the place was guessed as "maybe where the airport is now." "No! No!" shouted a good part of the audience.

They were among those who came to see an old film of Florence shot by a barnstorming filmmaker in 1935. They knew what they came to see and knew what they were seeing. The History Department at Francis Marion College sponsored the first showing in nearly twenty years of the film, reprinted on 16mm film from the old 35mm print that was a fire hazard in its later years.

Watching were some people who saw themselves, some who saw people and scenes they knew, some too young to remember and some who moved here in recent years and were anxious to get a look at how Florence looked in the mid-Depression.

One woman saw her father, who usually would not get in front of a camera, in one of the few pictures of him she had ever seen. One viewer commented that he could not believe anyone had made a film of Florence in 1935 that ran nearly an hour and did not include Frank Barnwell or Pete Thornell. He had a point.

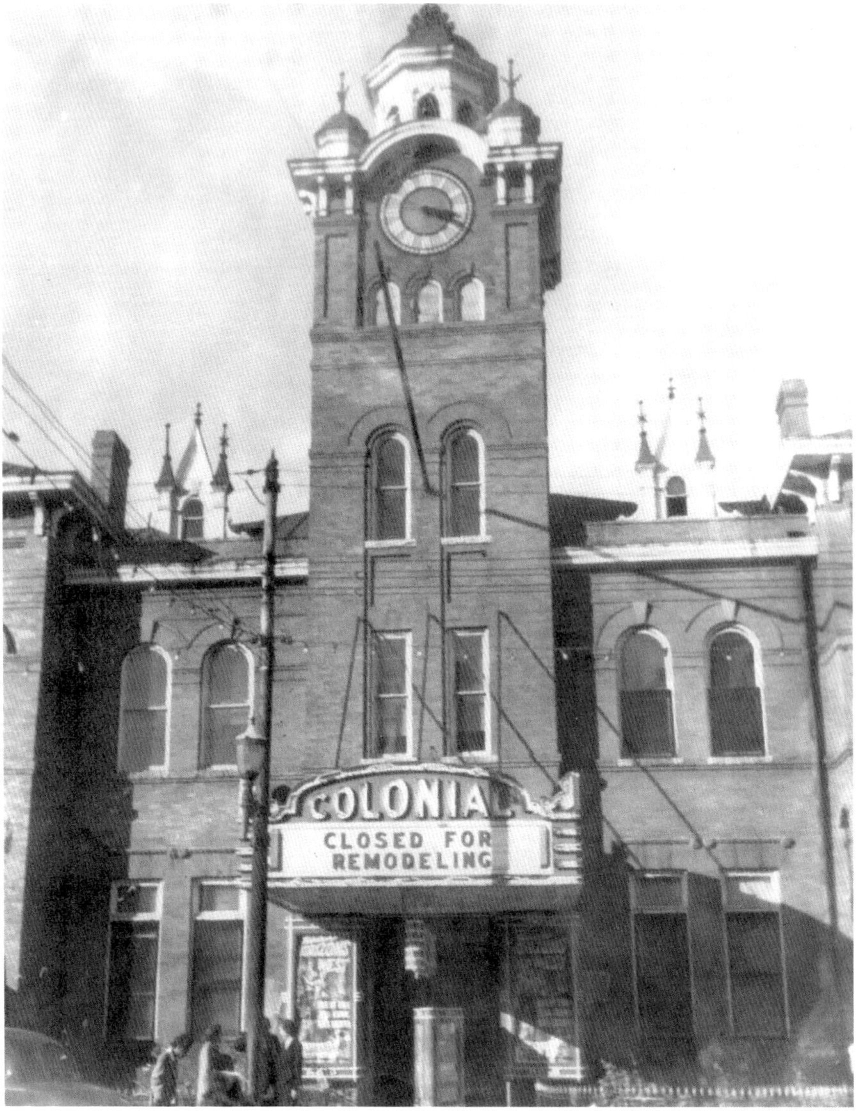

Old City Hall housed Colonial Theatre before it was replaced by a parking lot.

The film was of unusually good quality, and Mrs. Julia Schnibben, owner of the original, said that it was a "longtime dream" of herself and her late husband to have the film preserved. John Jebailey Jr. took a leading role in raising the $2,100 required to get the new prints made on safety film. One of the problems with the old one was that it was on an old, flammable film that would have been dangerous to show today. It was last shown in 1960, Mrs. Schnibben said, "and we held our breath then."

Two prints were made on safety film. One was given to Mrs. Schnibben and the other to the Florence Museum. The FMC Media Center made videocassettes, which will be available for viewing by appointment.

Primitive equipment is featured in the part of the film that shows work going on in the old Evans Street plant of the *Morning News*. Having been a kid with the run of the plant in the late 1930s, I saw a lot of people I remembered. I particularly liked the tiny flatbed press they showed in operation in the basement. The *Morning News* has had three presses since that one. A more modern flatbed press with a sixteen-page, two-section capacity was put in on the main floor a year or two after that film was made. Then, when the paper moved to the present Irby Street building in the late 1940s, a thirty-two-page capacity press was purchased. About the mid-1960s, a separate printing plant was built on Railroad Avenue and a sixty-four-page, four-section capacity press was put in. We still use that one.

The cameras went to the old school on the 100 block of East Cheves Street that was torn down about forty years ago. They also went to Poynor Junior High, which was not yet under that name; McClenaghan Junior High, which was merely "the high school"; McKenzie School, then Circle School; and Harllee School, then Park School. Harllee School is being torn down now.

If you were in public schools then (and were white), chances are you are in the film. The filmmaker panned the entire student bodies of those schools, and the kids panned back.

There are not many exteriors of local buildings shown, but there are some good shots of the downtown area, showing funny-looking old cars and clothing styles. And it seems as if every single man in the film was smoking cigarettes vigorously.

I was glad to see the old fishponds that once were in front of the old Colonial Theatre, with statues of big frogs spitting water into the ponds and big real goldfish swimming around. It brought back a lot of memories for those who have memories going back that far. For the newcomers, it gives a little taste of what their present home was like years ago. Andrew Kampiziones, who accepted the print for the museum, said that it helps give people who moved here a better sense of roots.

2009 UPDATE: In 1979, the *Morning News*, as the column said, had had three presses since the one shown in the film. Now it has had two more presses and the office has moved from Irby to South Dargan Street. McClenaghan High School became a junior high school in 1979 and has been closed since then. Also, the Florence Museum has a copy of the film and the FMU Media Center has a video copy of the film.

Pros Hit Lake City Bank

A set of professionals came to Lake City quietly in 1934 and got little notice. They planned it that way. These pros had no certification from a university or other accrediting organization, and they had no formal credentials. It was early in the tobacco sales season, when Lake City was accustomed to seeing strange faces in town. It also was when Lake City banks would have more than the normal amount of cash, because of tobacco sales. The pros were bank robbers. They had a plan to get the job done quietly with no dramatic getaway or gunplay.

They invaded and took over the home of Palmetto State Bank president J. Hoyt Carter early on the morning of September 5, 1934. The Carter children were left bound and taped in the home while the robbers carried Mr. and Mrs. Carter to the bank before opening time and quietly took about $114,000. Arriving at the bank for work, cashier Fred Stalvey mistook the men with Carter for bank examiners, who sometimes appeared early in the day. He soon learned differently.

One of the men was Frank "Red" English, said to have had a connection to some of the famous Midwestern bank robbery gangs, such as Dillinger's. They stuffed the bank's money into pillowcases from the Carter home. They departed with Stalvey and the Carters as prisoners but released Mrs. Carter on the edge of town with a warning not to blow the whistle because they still had Stalvey and Carter. Mrs. Carter, fearing for her husband and Stalvey, did as she was told, saying nothing while rushing home to her children. They were all right.

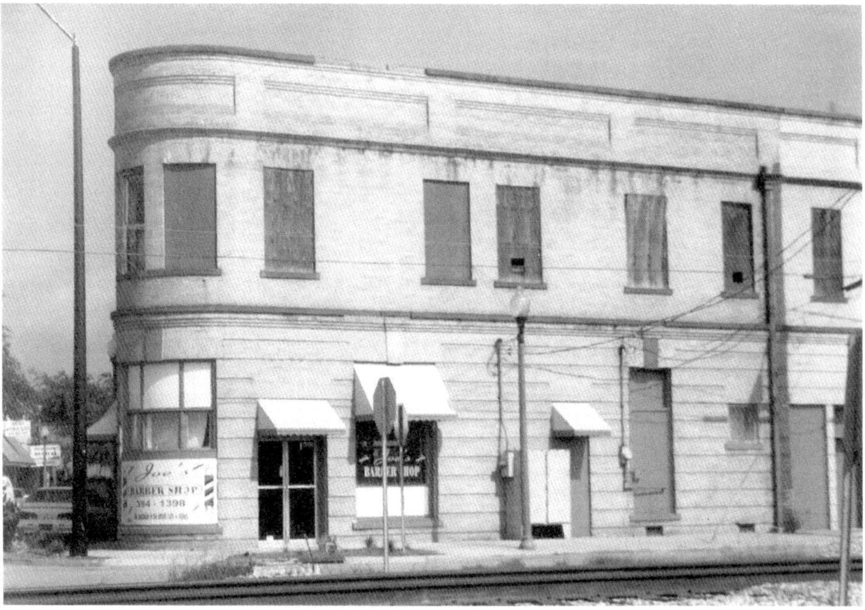

This Lake City building housed a bank that had an unusual robbery in the 1930s.

Her behavior was considered strange by some who saw her. Louis Propst told of encountering Mrs. Carter, who had always been very friendly. She more or less ignored him. "I thought it was strange," Propst said years later, "but I had no idea what was going on. It was a big surprise when I found out."

George Thomy reported a similar experience as he swept in front of a drugstore across Main Street from the bank. Mrs. Carter quickly passed and "didn't give any indication that she even saw me," which was very unusual. Later, from the drugstore where he worked, Thomy had a ringside view of the excitement after it was learned that the bank had been robbed.

English and his confederates told Stalvey and Carter that they would not be harmed, and they were not. They were released in the Lamar area, and it was learned later that the robbers had another car waiting for them near Hartsville. It turned out that the car used in Lake City had been stolen from a Florence cab driver the night before. The plotters had asked to be taken to a tourist court but forcibly took the car.

A statewide manhunt was staged, but the robbers escaped the state. However, acting on a tip, a little later police arrested English and his wife, who also had been involved, in Louisville, Kentucky. They were brought to South Carolina, where he was housed in the state penitentiary and she in the Florence County jail.

The Englishes went on trial on April 1, 1935, in Florence, where heavily armed lawmen stood guard. It was feared that some of the gangs with whom English was said to be affiliated might try to free him.

He first tried to defend himself but later depended on defense counsel, which included Cole Blease, a former governor. English changed his plea to guilty shortly after the trial started. He was sentenced to five years for breaking and entering, twenty for kidnapping and twenty-five for burglary of a bank, apparently to be served concurrently, because the judge said that South Carolina would be responsible for him for twenty-five years and then "you will be turned over to the state of Texas where they will have to be responsible for the next twenty-five years of your life." English had escaped from a Texas prison where he was serving a term for homicide.

His wife argued that she was not really a participant but had gone along because of her fear of him. She was found guilty of lesser charges and sentenced to one year, which was served in the Florence County jail. She quickly became a trusty and apparently was pretty well liked. It was said that she never ate jailhouse food.

There must have been a sort of gallantry about the gang members. They apparently did not hurt anybody physically, and they gave Mrs. Carter a couple of dollars to replace pillowcases they took from the home. They gave Carter and Stalvey five dollars each to help them get home after their release. When they stole the cab, they assured the cabbie that the car would not be damaged and would be easy to find later. Afterward, the cab driver displayed the car in Florence, drawing big crowds.

The $114,000 they got was much more money in 1934 than it would be in the twenty-first century, but it was not lost to the Lake City citizens. Insurance covered the bank's loss, and the depositors still had their money.

Kids Find Crashed Airliner

Military planes and a navy blimp flew over the Pee Dee swamp near Mars Bluff early on September 8, 1945. They sought an Eastern Airlines plane that, hours earlier, had radioed that it was having difficulty and planned to land at the Florence Army Air Field, and then disappeared. (FAAF was the Florence municipal airport before the Army Air Corps took it over during World War II; now it is the Florence Regional Airport.)

Two young Harwell boys, Hicks, age twelve, and David, age fourteen, and a neighbor, Joe Johnson, watched the planes and blimp behind the Harwell home on the Old Marion Highway. They had heard that a plane might be down in the area. As it turned out, the crash was on their family's property, about two miles from their home.

Hicks Harwell said that he and Johnson were fishing and watching the circling aircraft when "I told Joe, I'll bet they are looking for that airplane." He said they were carrying a nice string of fish and riding horses along a fence that separated the farm from the swamp. David was close by.

"I thought I saw fog," Hicks said, "and Joe said, no, it's smoke." Then Hicks was first to see the plane, his attention drawn by the glare of sunlight reflecting on metal. They made their way through brush and water and found that the glare came from a wing. At first they couldn't see the fuselage, but they alerted David. "I climbed over a fence to get to the plane and looked to see if anyone was still living. They were all dead," David wrote in 1945.

"It was a right horrible thing to look at," David said. "Body parts were scattered around. The wreckage covered fifty yards or so." Both Harwells recalled more than sixty years later that the worst thing was smelling "burning flesh."

The crash was big news the next day. One article described the plane as "a huge Eastern Airliner." (It was a two-engine DC-3, famed as a military workhorse during World War II. But it carried only twenty-two people, less than huge in the twenty-first century.)

The *Morning News* reported the next morning that the plane had been traveling from Miami to New York. It was on a leg from Savannah to Raleigh when a problem developed. The pilot apparently had turned back toward the Florence airport when he crashed in heavy woods that made it difficult to spot from the air.

News reports were unclear on what the problem was, but there was speculation that there was fire aboard while the plane was airborne. The plane's stabilizer was burned, but a tree that fell on it was not burned, which strengthened the belief that it had burned in the air.

One body was reported not burned. That was a man who had been thrown clear of the wreckage but apparently died from blows to the head.

The next day, David Harwell had a byline story on the Associated Press wire describing the experience. He said that the plane was smoldering and there were "lots of bodies." It must have been carrying airmail, because many letters were scattered among clothing and other items from baggage.

Upon their discovery, the young boys alerted their mother, who called the Florence Army Air Field, and Army Air Corps personnel arrived in a matter of minutes.

The Harwells said that their grandmother had heard the crash during the night, a little after 2:00 a.m., but their mother had thought it was just thunder. "When planes stared circling in the sky about 9 o'clock, I knew there must have been a plane crash. That's when we started looking for it." Hicks Harwell recalled in 2009 that one engine was buried deep in the mud in the swampy area about three miles from the Pee Dee River. "The tail and one wing I walked on was about all you could see."

He said that the army took the engine out and left most of the plane. People took the metal out later and sold it for scrap. "After they took the bodies out," Hicks Harwell said, "I went back and saw that pine trees were stripped at the top where it went in," and some trees and underbrush around the plane were burned.

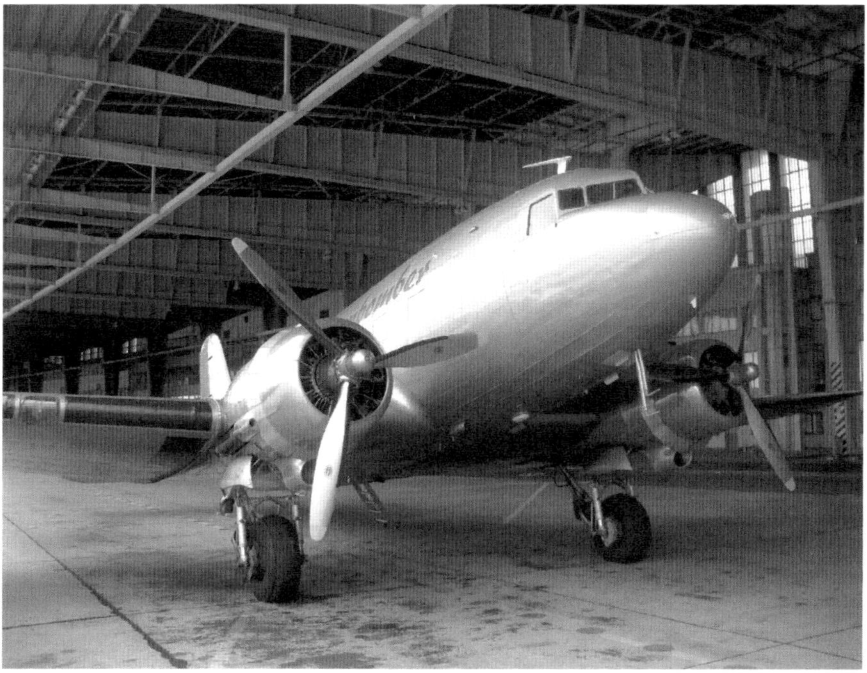

A DC3 of the type that crashed in the Pee Dee River swamp, shown in a hangar. *Courtesy of the Library of Congress.*

A makeshift road was built to get motor vehicles as close as possible to the crash site, but he said that they used horses, tractors and wagons to bring bodies part of the way out. The "road" ran about three-quarters of a mile to get ambulances and military vehicles close.

News reports said that most of the charred bodies were found in a heap near the center of the wreckage, but others were scattered. Bodies were taken to Florence, where identifications were made. Of the twenty-two people aboard, nine were armed forces personnel, ten were civilian passengers and three were crew.

Eddie Rickenbacker, president and general manager of Eastern Airlines, said that the company was at a loss to explain the crash, noting that the country is level and there was a ceiling of more than six thousand feet. The plane left Miami at 9:00 p.m., had taken off from Savannah at 12:30 a.m. and went down about 2:00 a.m.

A statement from the commander of the Florence field said that planes from Chatham Field, Savannah; Charleston Army Air Base; and army planes from Florence; Laurinburg-Maxton, North Carolina; Wilmington, North Carolina; and Pope Field at Fort Bragg were involved in the air search. He said that poor visibility and the fact that the wreckage was "almost totally hidden by the air from surrounding trees" made it difficult to spot from the air.

The *Morning News* carried a separate story on the activities of an Associated Press photographer who flew in from Atlanta. He worked out of the newspaper office that then was on East Evans Street, and the story said that the Harwells helped him get to the scene by horseback. The Harwell boys were credited with helping many of the military and government personnel make their way through the swampy area, some by horseback and some on foot.

Hicks said that he went back to the scene a few years later but primarily has wanted to forget it.

Both Harwells went into politics and the judiciary years later. Both served in the state House of Representatives, and both served as circuit judges. David served on the state supreme court and retired as chief justice.

More Thrill than Planned

A Carolina Theatre ad promised the "most amazing thrill" on November 17, 1939. It was not kidding. Showing was *San Francisco*, a drama centered on the West Coast city's earthquake of 1906. Much had been said about the film's depiction of the earthquake and fire. It was much anticipated in Florence, but here the drama would not be confined to the screen.

About four hundred people were in the theatre. Some said that it was during the fire sequence when the house lights went up and a young theatre usher named Woodrow Cook went down front. He announced that state law required fire drills at theaters, and one had been ordered for this theatre. If everyone filed out quickly, he explained, when the inspectors saw that the theatre had been emptied, they could return and finish the movie. It was an orderly evacuation, but when the audience reached Dargan Street, they were astonished to find smoke billowing from the roof. The Carolina Theatre was burning.

Cook had noticed smoke and flashes of flame in the upper reaches of the theatre just before calling on the audience to file out. While Cook was going down front, a phone call was made to Martin Schnibben, manager of the Carolina and Colonial Theatres, Florence's two main movie houses. "Mr. Cluck is at the Carolina," Schnibben was told. He hung up and hurried from his office at the Colonial to the Carolina.

"Mr. Cluck" was theatre management code for fire, so the call told Schnibben that there was a fire at the Carolina. The last thing theatre workers wanted was panic, and shouting "fire" in a crowded theatre is considered the ultimate panic-generating act.

The *Morning News* reported the next day that fire quickly spread from underneath the balcony "to the roof until it became a blazing mass." About fifteen minutes later, the roof crashed into the theatre.

The Florence Fire Department came, and witnesses remember firefighting equipment all over the 100 block of South Dargan Street and smoke pouring from the theatre. The newspaper reported that the firemen could do little but prevent fire spreading throughout the business district. The theatre was quickly lost.

The "fire drill" served its purpose. The audience filed out quickly and in good order. There were no casualties. An African American family who lived in an apartment above the projection booth escaped unharmed.

One audience member said that she had never heard of a practice fire drill, "so I thought something was wrong, but we went on out." When they got outside, she said the first things they saw were fire trucks and more arriving. "We just stood around outside, and it was very orderly. I think they may have given us our money back, but I'm not sure."

Another young girl that day recalled that "there was no panic" as the theatre was emptied. Outside, she remembered being "bewildered" by the fire trucks and excitement.

The *Florence Evening Star*, an afternoon paper at the time, came out shortly after the fire started. It reported that spread of the fire seemed likely. Waters Furniture Co. was next door, and the *Star* said, "Only a miracle can save Waters from serious damage." It said that the firewall between the theatre and the store was "cracking under the heat." The *Star* had more than a passing interest. The newspaper's offices were a few doors down Dargan from the theatre. As its pressmen printed that afternoon, they must have smelled the smoke.

Volunteers helped the firefighters, though at times curious people got in the way. The Darlington Fire Department helped contain the fire and avoided repetition of fires that, decades before, had wiped out much of the Florence business district. In 1939, some people remembered the earlier fires.

Concentrating on protecting neighboring stores, the fire department played water on Waters and Oulla's Furniture Co., which were on either side of the theatre. Those stores had some minor damage, but that was about it. The required "miracle" the *Star* had mentioned saved Waters.

Ernest Oulla, in Danville, Virginia, on a business trip, learned of the fire by phone and hurriedly returned to Florence. Marion Waters used a fire extinguisher to stop a fire developing on the roof of the Waters store.

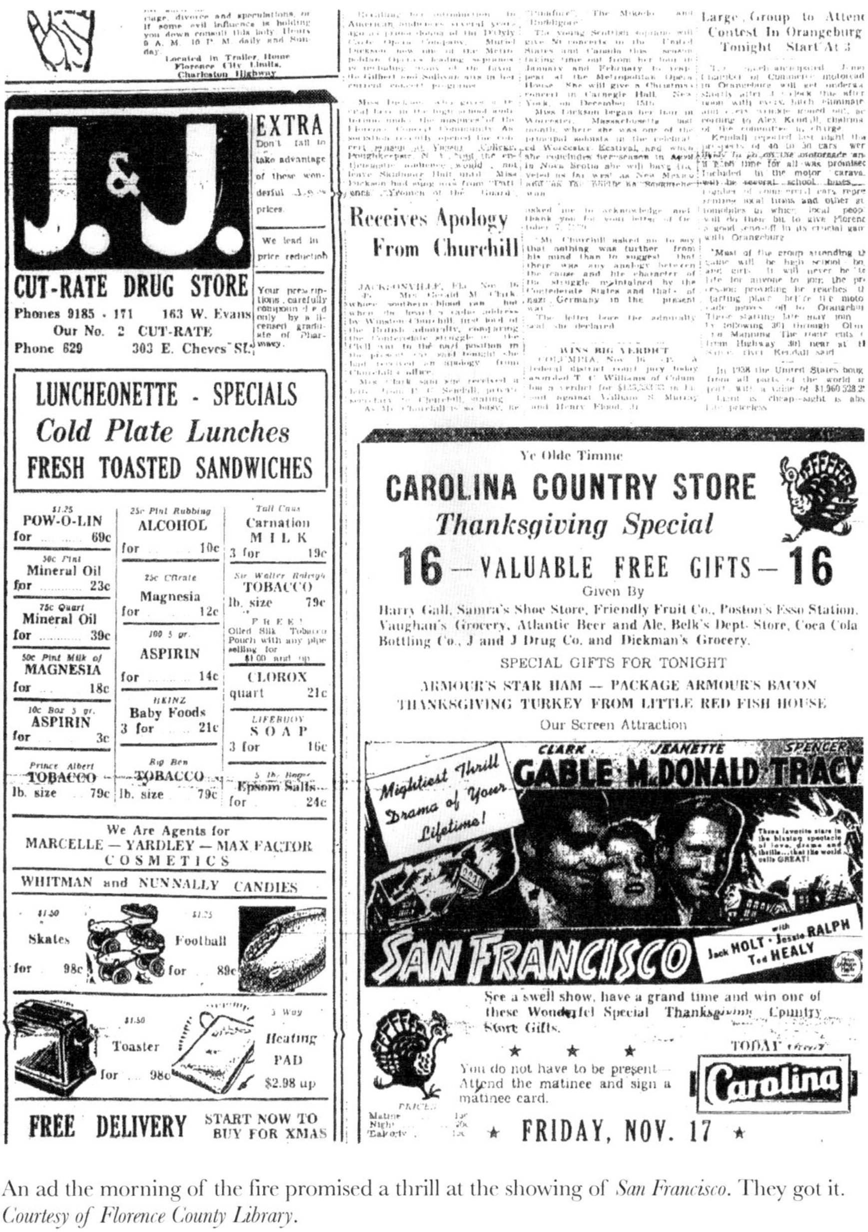
Located in Trailer Home
Florence City Limits,
Charleston Highway

J. & J.
EXTRA
Don't fail to take advantage of these wonderful prices.
We lead in price reduction
CUT-RATE DRUG STORE
Your prescriptions carefully compounded only by a licensed graduate of Pharmacy.
Phones 9185 - 171 163 W. Evans
Our No. 2 CUT-RATE
Phone 629 303 E. Cheves St.

LUNCHEONETTE - SPECIALS
Cold Plate Lunches
FRESH TOASTED SANDWICHES

$1.25 POW-O-LIN for 69c
25c Pint Rubbing ALCOHOL for 10c
Tall Cans Carnation MILK 3 for 19c
50c Pint Mineral Oil for 23c
25c Citrate Magnesia for 12c
Sir Walter Raleigh TOBACCO lb. size 79c
75c Quart Mineral Oil for 39c
100 5 gr. ASPIRIN for 14c
50c Pint Milk of MAGNESIA for 18c
CLOROX quart 21c
10c Box 5 gr. ASPIRIN for 3c
HEINZ Baby Foods 3 for 21c
LIFEBUOY SOAP 3 for 16c
Prince Albert TOBACCO lb. size 79c
Big Ben TOBACCO lb. size 79c
Epsom Salts for 24c

We Are Agents for
MARCELLE — YARDLEY — MAX FACTOR
COSMETICS
WHITMAN and NUNNALLY CANDIES

$1.50 Skates for 98c
$1.25 Football for 89c
$1.50 Toaster for 98c
3 Way Heating PAD $2.98 up
FREE DELIVERY
START NOW TO BUY FOR XMAS

Receives Apology From Churchill

Large Group to Attend Contest In Orangeburg Tonight Start At 3

Ye Olde Timme
CAROLINA COUNTRY STORE
Thanksgiving Special
16 — VALUABLE FREE GIFTS — 16
Given By
Harry Gall, Samra's Shoe Store, Friendly Fruit Co., Poston's Esso Station, Vaughan's Grocery, Atlantic Beer and Ale, Belk's Dept. Store, Coca Cola Bottling Co., J and J Drug Co. and Dickman's Grocery.
SPECIAL GIFTS FOR TONIGHT
ARMOUR'S STAR HAM — PACKAGE ARMOUR'S BACON
THANKSGIVING TURKEY FROM LITTLE RED FISH HOUSE
Our Screen Attraction
Mightiest Thrill Drama of Your Lifetime!
CLARK GABLE JEANETTE MacDONALD SPENCER TRACY
SAN FRANCISCO
with Jack HOLT · Jessie RALPH · Ted HEALY
See a swell show, have a grand time and win one of these Wonderful Special Thanksgiving Country Store Gifts.
★ ★ ★
You do not have to be present — Attend the matinee and sign a matinee card.
TODAY
Carolina
FRIDAY, NOV. 17

An ad the morning of the fire promised a thrill at the showing of *San Francisco*. They got it. *Courtesy of Florence County Library.*

The fire department was praised for containing the fire, but nobody got more praise than Cook, the young usher who calmly announced the "practice" fire drill and led the successful evacuation. Grover C. Hinds, commander of the local VFW post, praised Cook's actions and said that the youth deserved a medal "if anybody did." The VFW and American Legion said they would recommend Cook for a Carnegie Medal, but that apparently did not happen. However, not long after that, *Reader's Digest* carried a piece on Cook's actions, giving him national recognition. As for Cook, he joined the volunteers who helped the firemen and then went home, changed clothes and reported for work at the Colonial Theatre that night.

The next day, a man wore his badly damaged hat that had been recovered from the wreckage. It was "a total loss." A woman showed up seeking her gloves that had been left inside as the building was evacuated. "If I thought they were fooling me, I would have brought them out," she said.

An ad in the *Morning News* signed by C.D. Waters, manager of Waters Furniture Co., said, "We want to take this opportunity publicly to thank the firemen who worked diligently to save our building from serious damage. We will open for business as usual today." An editorial praised the firemen.

Schnibben estimated the loss at $35,000 and pledged that the Carolina would be rebuilt, much better and bigger. Rebuilding would take sixty to ninety days, he estimated. As it turned out, it took a little longer. The rebuilt theatre opened on April 1, 1940. An additional thirty feet of property at the rear was bought, and the stage was smaller, since it no longer planned vaudeville shows. Dressing rooms backstage were eliminated and that space was used for more seating. It was stressed that the new theatre would be fireproof, mostly built with concrete and steel. "Safe" was a word that came up frequently about the rebuilding project. Once the new marquee was up, it read, "The new Carolina will open April 1. No fooling."

Colonel Frank Barnwell, a Florence businessman and character, presided at the reopening ceremonies, and Mayor Pro Tem Rowland Zeigler represented the city, using "well-chosen words," according to news reports.

The Carolina went into the second half of the twentieth century before being sold to a chain that renamed it the Cinema Five and operated it for several years as the downtown declined. It later became known as Theater One and, still later, housed meetings and church services.

It remains there, mostly unoccupied. In 2008, a proposal was made to turn it into a mini-brewery.

Helen's Great Voyage

R.E. Hanna had a dream. Head of the South Carolina Economic Association, he believed that revival of riverboat service on the Pee Dee River would give the area an economic boost. For one thing, he believed that reestablishment of river freight service would mean improved railroad rates. The association sought redevelopment of the channel between Georgetown and Cheraw, but nothing had happened. It got encouragement from points along the river, particularly development-minded Florence.

The group decided to go ahead and move some freight up the river as it was and prove that, with development, river traffic was viable. That was when the *Helen*, a Charleston Harbor tugboat, entered the picture. The plan was for the *Helen* to take a barge from Charleston to Cheraw through the Intracoastal Waterway to Georgetown and up the Pee Dee to Cheraw, delivering freight on a route that had not seen such service since about World War I.

On February 26, 1939, the *Helen* set out from Charleston. It would be a great adventure. If anything turned out as planned, it is not recorded.

Things went well as far as Georgetown but became more difficult after turning onto the river. Rainfall had been heavy in the Pee Dee drainage area. The *Helen* faced a swift current as it plodded upstream. Far behind schedule, the *Helen* stopped near Hemingway for the night. From there, Hanna made a little journey to Florence to boost news coverage. He waded a great distance through shallow flooding to a farmhouse, from which he walked to a road to hitchhike. He finally made it to Florence.

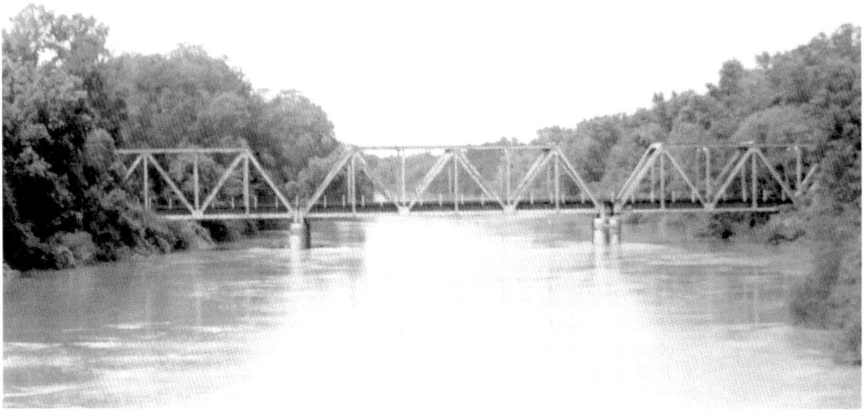

A railroad bridge over the Pee Dee River at Pee Dee delayed *Helen* on its trip back to Charleston.

Hanna made his news contacts there; the next day, he went to the Pee Dee community to meet the *Helen*. Besides the Pee Dee newspapers, Hanna's association produced a newsletter and a statewide radio program that spread the word. News coverage generated enough excitement that several hundred people were at the Mars Bluff bridge to see the boat arrive.

A boat like the *Helen* had not been seen before on the river. Riverboats that old-timers remembered were much different. The swift current had proved more than the boat could handle with the barge, so the barge was left behind, probably near Hemingway. Oil bound for Cheraw was moved from the barge to the *Helen*.

Hanna apparently re-boarded the boat at Pee Dee. It struggled to Society Hill and picked up some furniture from a plant there, bound for Cheraw. Finally, the *Helen* reached Cheraw, where it created quite a stir. It was exciting for that town, which had been an important river port before the railroads. At Cheraw, the *Helen* took on a load of bricks bound for a building project at The Citadel.

Returning with the current was easier, and the boat boarded another load of furniture at Society Hill, bound for Pee Dee, from where it would go to a Florence furniture store.

Then the *Helen* encountered another problem: the river had so risen that the boat could not get under the railroad bridge at Pee Dee. Once it had been a drawbridge but was no longer. After a few days, the water level dropped, and the *Helen* continued downstream, picking up the barge in Hemingway or wherever they had left it.

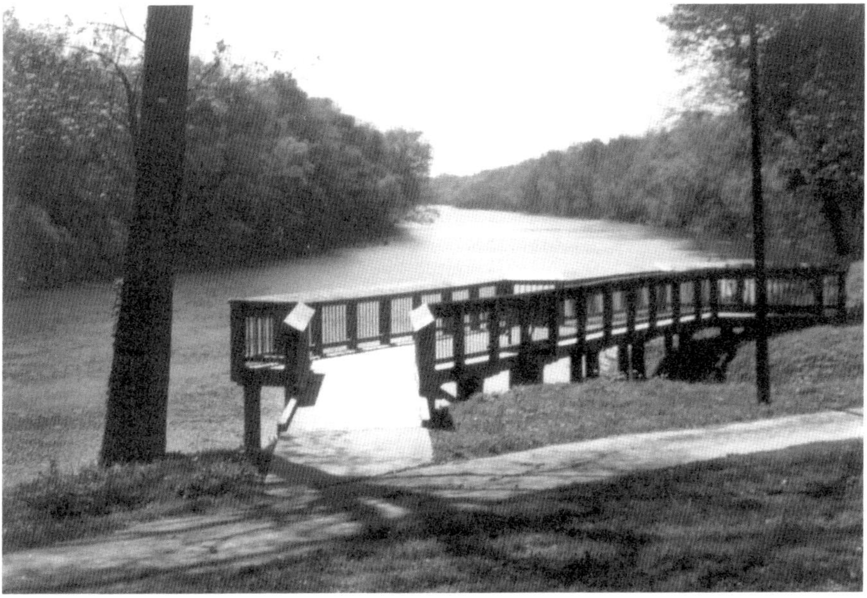

A city park on the Pee Dee River bank at Cheraw was *Helen*'s destination.

The *Helen* returned to Charleston on March 11 and delivered the bricks to The Citadel. Hanna's son, R.E. Hanna Jr., a cadet there, helped unload them. The younger Hanna later recalled from California that his father and the South Carolina Economic Association were enthusiastic about reviving shipping on the rivers, like the Savannah, Congaree and Santee, believing that it would boost the state's economy. The Pee Dee was not the only river they were interested in, but only the Pee Dee had the *Helen*.

River development was taken seriously. Bills in the state legislature tried to help, as did congressmen. There were congressional hearings on Pee Dee River traffic, one in Florence as late as 1965.

As for the Pee Dee trip, Hanna spoke optimistically about it. He pointed to the flooding of the river and heavy rainfall encountered by the *Helen* and said that they proved "water transportation…to be an all-weather method." He said there was plenty of water between Mars Bluff and Cheraw to support river traffic. He argued that, with development, the water flow would maintain a viable channel from Cheraw to Pee Dee, and below Mars Bluff, all was fine.

Cheraw looked back fondly on riverboat history. The town listed several names of riverboats that once worked the river. Old-timers could recall occasions when the dock area, now a city park, was visited by several boats at once. Hundreds of thousands of bales of cotton were shipped from Cheraw. In St. David's churchyard in Cheraw is the grave of Mose Rogers, who operated a riverboat after becoming famous as captain of the USS *Savannah*, the first steamship to cross the Atlantic. On a trip up the Pee Dee, he died of yellow fever.

Newspapers and chambers of commerce backed the project and put a good face on the *Helen*'s efforts. A.B. Jordan of Dillon was a passenger early in the trip. He was enthusiastic, and he wrote in his *Dillon Herald* about riding from Charleston to Georgetown and hitting a sandbar on that run. Jordan argued that river transportation would relieve the highways, which were "already overcrowded with large trucks."

Business interests along the Pee Dee River route remained enthusiastic after the voyage, and the *Morning News*, which had been a cheerleader, joined the chorus, saying that the *Helen*'s adventure proved river freight service workable.

Preston Charles, a columnist for the Florence paper, was not as enthusiastic. He suggested that the organizers should have consulted the weather bureau rather than local promoters. "Almost any time this winter would have been better than this particular week," he wrote.

Soon, any momentum that the *Helen*'s heroic effort had created was swept away when World War II started. After the war, the nation's resources turned more toward highways and air travel. There was more conversation but little done to reestablish Pee Dee riverboat traffic.

The *Helen* later was sunk to become part of a fishing reef off the coast, but not because of the trip to Cheraw.

Fatal Flight Home

Marion Huggins of Timmonsville was a young man with a bright future. In the 1920s, the *Morning News* carried a story and picture when he was one of four West Point honor graduates. He went into the army and became a pilot. In 1937, he was promoted to captain, and that June he served as operations officer at the Army Air Corps Maxwell Field in Alabama.

It was convenient that his youngest brother, Thad Huggins, a student at the University of Georgia Law School, was doing ROTC training nearby at Fort McClellan when they learned that their mother was critically ill in Timmonsville. Captain Huggins used an army airplane to fly home and picked up his brother on the way. They would arrive together to cheer up their mother, creating a nice, warm family scene. It did not work out that way.

On June 26, 1937, according to the *Morning News*, Timmonsville people "glanced up admiringly at a huge yellow-winged government pursuit plane as it banked to salute them." The plane flew over the Hugginses' home on Brockington Street and banked toward the nearby landing field when witnesses said that "the motor appeared to slow and went dead about 1,000 feet from the ground." It was nearly in sight of their home.

Witnesses said that the plane spun and fell toward a residential area. The pilot apparently tried to guide it to an uninhabited area but could not make it. It was headed into a vacant lot on Clifford Street when it hit and broke utility lines. It went down there, and the brothers were dead on impact.

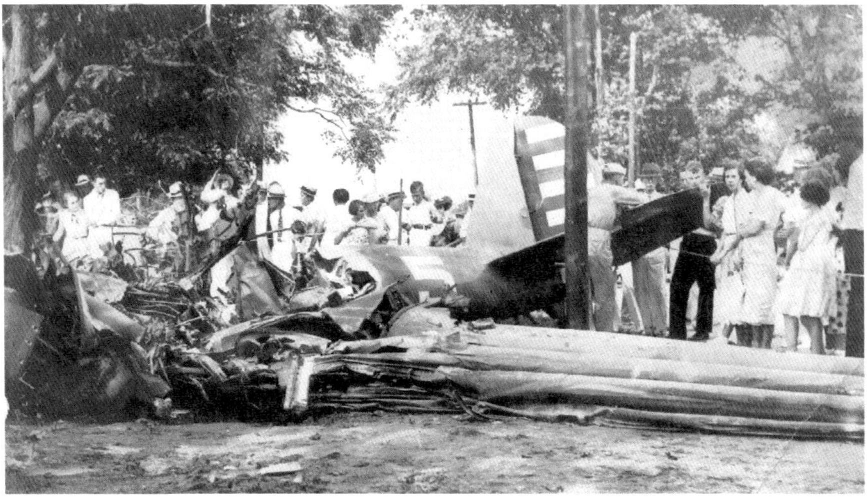

Crowds take a look at the 1930s plane crash in a Timmonsville residential area. *Courtesy of Betty Huggins McAllister.*

Another pilot who was landing at the Timmonsville airstrip at the time said that the plane never recovered from the turn toward the airfield.

News reports first said that Thad was thrown clear, but later said that both bodies were trapped in the plane. The wreckage was so twisted that an auto wrecker was required to pull it apart to remove the bodies.

The crash site was about a block from the grammar school, a couple of blocks from Main Street, so a crowd quickly developed. First to arrive were the chief of police and a county magistrate. Among the first was the victims' oldest brother, M.B. Huggins Jr.

The scene quickly was roped off, and people were warned not to smoke because of heavy gasoline fumes. Equipment arrived quickly and the bodies were removed. That was good, because about an hour afterward, fire broke out and the plane burned. Smoking was suspected. Army guards were posted until the army could investigate. The Timmonsville tragedy was front-page news statewide.

Dr. James McLeod came from Florence to attend to Mrs. Huggins, who was not told immediately about the tragedy, and other family members.

Marion Huggins's death sent shock waves throughout the army. He was a popular officer with a great future. He had served in the United States and the Philippines and already had had instances when mechanical problems had given him aerial emergencies to deal with. He had done so successfully until Timmonsville.

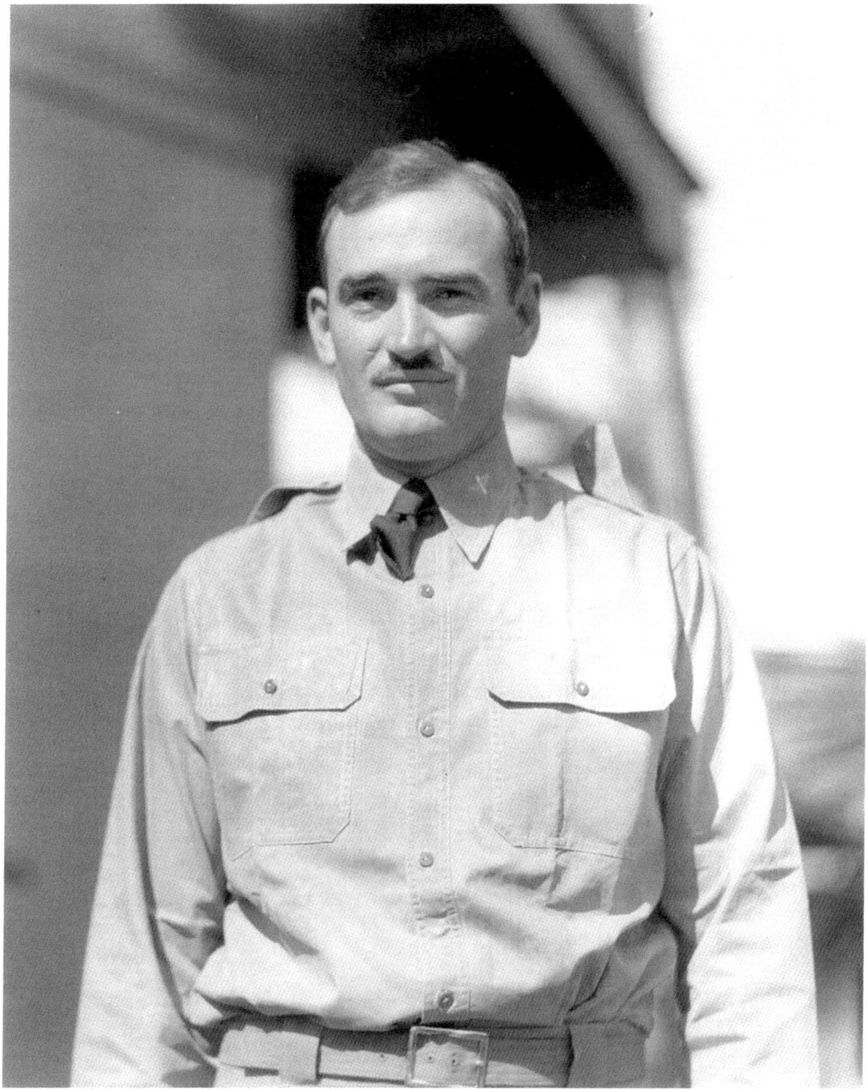

Marion Huggins. *Courtesy of Betty Huggins McAllister.*

Their father, M.B. Huggins Sr., was a respected Timmonsville businessman who was serving in the state House of Representatives. There was a great outpouring of sympathy from around the state and the military community.

The military suggested burial at Arlington National Cemetery, but the family overruled that and scheduled the service and burial in Timmonsville.

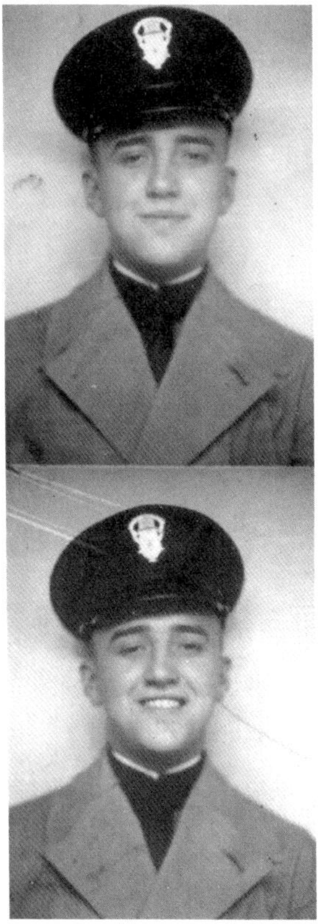

Thad Huggins. *Courtesy of Betty Huggins McAllister.*

It started at the Huggins home so that Mrs. Huggins, who by then had been informed of the tragedy, could attend that part of the service. Then, with an honor guard of army and National Guard units from Timmonsville and Florence, the procession moved to Byrd Cemetery while a squadron of army planes circled. The part of the service held at the home could accommodate only a small number of people, but it was estimated that thousands turned out for the procession and the cemetery portion. Governor Olin D. Johnston came to Timmonsville, as did the commander of Maxwell Field. There was a twenty-one-gun salute in three volleys, and a bugler played Taps in the distance.

Until the wreckage was cleared, many curious people came to Timmonsville, and a large number of people were without power for a period after the crash knocked down power lines.

Witnesses thought that the controls must have been jammed because Captain Huggins could have steered the plane into open space nearer their home for an emergency landing

Marion Huggins was a cadet at Clemson College when he got an appointment to West Point in 1923. He went into the army as a second lieutenant in 1927, and in 1929 he transferred to the Air Corps.

Thad Huggins had been a cadet at The Citadel before going to law school at the University of Georgia. He was an ROTC air cadet at his death.

Young Businessmen

Morning News column, 1980

When I was in junior high school, these little comic books were a popular item. They were unauthorized adventures of some of the popular comic strip characters of the day taking part in activities not included in the regular strips in the daily newspaper. I particularly remember a couple of them. You would never have pictured Blondie doing what she did in those little comic books. And Minnie Mouse, for Pete's sake.

Anyway, they sold for a quarter from beneath the counter of a service station not far from the junior high school that had not yet been named for Parson Poynor. A couple of service station attendants were the local outlet for these little books that were a hot item in the boys' restroom at school. I understand they created interest in the girls' room, too.

Some of us around the neighborhood combined our resources to buy a few of the books. A quarter was a lot of money then, buying, among other things, a gallon of gasoline.

We had a stroke of genius. We put carbon paper between sheets of white paper and thumbtacked the dirty little comic books, a page at a time, over the blank white sheets. Then we traced the comics and made about four or five copies. The copies were crude, but then, so was the subject matter. We put them together with straight pins since no stapler was available, making new little comic books. Our price of ten cents a copy was a real bargain compared to the quarter the originals were going for.

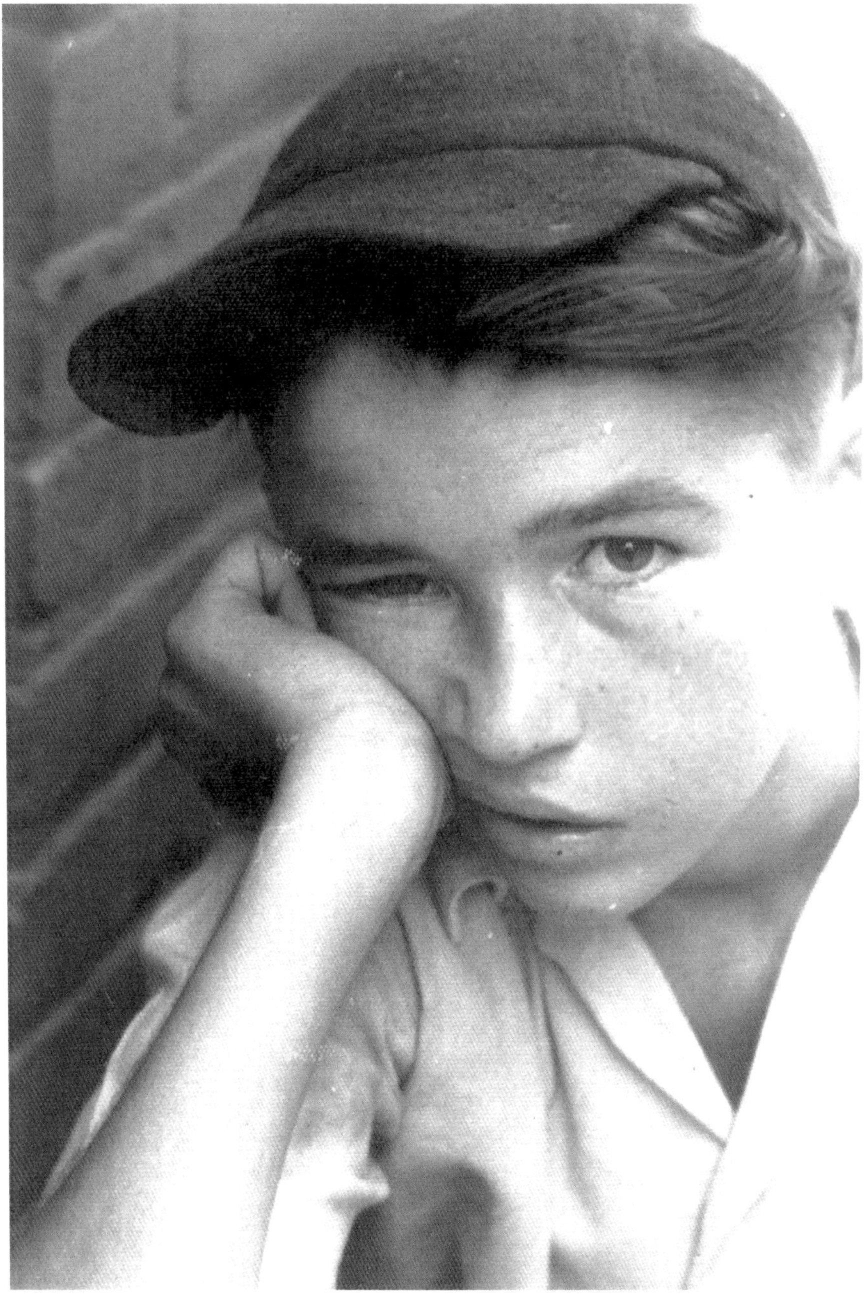

A young businessman (the writer). *Courtesy of George McDaniel Jr.*

Things went well for a while, and we picked up a little pocket money as well as the reputation of being the teenybopper porn kings of Gregg Avenue. Then one day I dropped by the filling station to pick up a new original, and a stoolie had told the big guys who sold them what we were up to. Not only did one of them refuse to sell me another, but he also offered me a deal I could not refuse—quit making copies or suffer assorted cuts, breaks and bruises.

He talked like he meant it. He acted like he meant it. I think he did mean it. I left the porn business at a much younger age than most people get into it—before Larry Flynt even thought about it.

I guess writing a newspaper column is a good substitute.

Times do change, you know. Those things were considered quite an outrage at the time. Now similar stuff would barely get a yawn.

"March of Dimes" Jones

Morning News column, August 22, 2004

Many drivers nowadays probably notice the name of James Jones Avenue and wonder for whom it was named. The answer is one of Florence's best stories.

In the 1920s, a black Florence youth saw his sweetheart die of polio, a disease that struck fear into the hearts of Florence parents because it seemed to particularly target young people. The youth was James Jones, and as his sweetheart suffered, he promised that he would do something to combat this disease. However, what could a young fellow who had dropped out of school at age twelve to help support his family and with no prospect of getting an education do to fight polio?

In a few years, he had his answer. President Franklin D. Roosevelt, himself a victim of the disease, established the March of Dimes, which was dedicated to raising big money in small amounts to combat polio. Jones would raise money for the March of Dimes.

It must have seemed presumptuous in those days of strict segregation for a young black man to go around town asking people for money, no matter what he said was his purpose. But Jones, who became well known in Florence both as a Western Union deliveryman and red cap at the Atlantic Coast Line Railroad station, had a good reputation, and people were impressed with his sincerity and dedication.

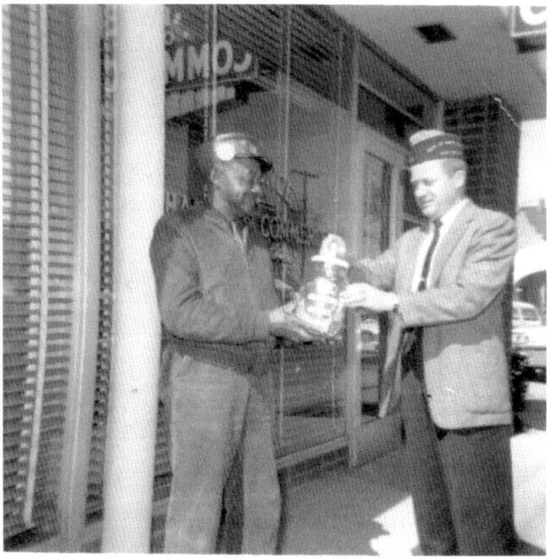

James Jones receives a donation to the March of Dimes from state commander of the VFW Bill Brown. *Courtesy of Norma Phillips.*

The first year, 1938, he collected $102.10. In the 1930s, the dollar was worth much more than today, so the total made a nice contribution to the March of Dimes.

Each year he scheduled his vacations so that he could devote more time to the drive. He placed jars in businesses around town to receive donations and traveled miles around the city by bike, carrying a jar that he asked people to fill with donations.

His annual one-man drive grew into hundreds, then thousands, then tens of thousands of dollars. Others took up his cause and collected funds to turn over to his campaign. His high yearly total was $13,894.87, and it was estimated that in thirty-three campaigns, he raised more than $231,000. In 2004 dollars, this would be in seven figures.

Eventually, he took the campaign as a nickname and was widely known as James "March of Dimes" Jones. During drives, he was seen on his bike with a jacket bearing that famous name.

He also was famed for his autograph collection, and he liked to describe how it started. Will Rogers made an appearance in Florence, and Jones delivered a telegram to him. For a tip, Rogers gave Jones an autograph book, saying that when someone gave you his autograph, he gave you part of himself. Rogers gave the young man his first autograph. Jones collected thousands of autographs, probably including most people in town. I even remember signing one for him myself. Mine was not the most distinguished he had.

He had governors, senators, presidents, movie stars and sports heroes. Florence people who met famous people often brought autographs back for Jones's collection. It even was said that a Florence resident who attended the Berlin Olympics in 1936 contributed Hitler's. Many of the autographs came from Jones's access to ACL trains as a red cap. The famous people of the time often traveled through Florence by rail.

About 1970, James Jones lost his eyesight to diabetes, and his crusade slowed. He died at age sixty-three on December 12, 1973. Mayor Cooper Tedder ordered flags on city buildings at half staff until the funeral and asked other organizations to do the same.

Jones collected well-earned recognition in his late years. Nationally syndicated columnist Drew Pearson designated Jones one of his Servants of Brotherhood. Florence civic clubs and state Knights of Columbus were among organizations that gave him honors.

On one of his last wedding anniversaries, the McClenaghan High School Chorale sang and the Southside High School Band played in front of the home of Mr. and Mrs. Jones.

Jonas Salk and Albert Sabin developed vaccines that provided immunity to polio. By the time of Jones's death, the disease was pretty much stamped out. It has been decades since it brought fear, when we as kids feared polio each summer and knew friends who were stricken, some fatally. When epidemics hit here, children often were banned from public gatherings like movies. I would wager that many children today have never even heard of polio. That is a very good thing. James Jones's efforts played a part in making that so.

The March of Dimes, with polio conquered, has turned to other projects, but James Jones's job was done, his crusade a success. He was one of Florence's finest and should be remembered.

Prisoners of War

Morning News column, August 23, 1978

During World War II, some German prisoners of war were held at the Army Air Corps base at the Florence municipal airport. They were used in work details by the army authorities, and arrangements were made for some of them to work on farms in the Florence area, easing the labor shortage that had been caused by the departure of many of the young men of the area.

Some of the prisoners worked on the farm of A.W. McLaughlin near Florence, and although they were soldiers from an enemy army, they got along well with the people for whom they were sent to work. The McLaughlin children got along famously with the prisoners, and they were particularly fond of Hans Mahr, a young Austrian who had been captured by American forces during the D-Day invasion of Normandy.

Soon after the war ended, the prisoners were sent back home. The McLaughlins got a letter or two from Hans and one of the others, but then lost touch, Mrs. McLaughlin recalled last week.

Her son, Lieutenant Colonel Robert H. McLaughlin, recently was transferred to Heidelberg, Germany, and "he said he was going to try to find Hans," she said, but he had no idea where to find him. McLaughlin went to a small Bavarian village where he had last known Mahr to be, asked about him and was quickly directed to a house down a lane. Down the lane he found a man and woman, asked for Hans Mahr and found that he was talking with Mahr and his wife.

When McLaughlin introduced himself, Mahr, now sixty-seven, was astonished. "He was very happy and remembered Robert as a boy," Mrs. McLaughlin said. "Robert was treated royally, and they called their twenty-five-year-old daughter who is an English teacher to interpret."

Mrs. McLaughlin said that Mahr produced a diary he had kept of the war years. His recollections were typed, and a lot of pictures were included in the book as illustrations. Among them were pictures of the McLaughlin family, scenes around the farm and other scenes around Florence.

McLaughlin has another former prisoner whom he plans to try to look up when he has a little time off, and he has an invitation to come back to Mahr's home, spend a little time and get to know the area better. McLaughlin wrote that Mahr lived in a small Bavarian village about the size of Effingham in a "beautiful Alpine chalet."

Mrs. McLaughlin said that she recalled having a good relationship with the prisoners who worked on their farm. "Hans was one of the crew of five who worked pretty regularly for us. At one time, they decided to shift the crews around and sent us some other people. The regulars were unhappy, the children were disappointed and we were unhappy," she said. After a little negotiation, they got their regular five back.

"We were not supposed to feed them or anything, but we did," she recalled. "We couldn't see them work the way they were and not have a little something to eat and drink. And when the time came for them to go back home after the war, we brought them in a night or two before they left and gave them a big dinner."

Hans's diary that her son recently saw mentioned the good treatment they had from the McLaughlins and recalled the incident when their work assignment was changed briefly. He reported in the diary that all of them were unhappy with the change and were pleased when they returned to the McLaughlins'.

2009 UPDATE: I recall having seen prisoners being transported around Florence. They had POW designations on them, as I remember, and usually I saw them on the backs of deuce-and-a-half trucks.

I also remember as about a sixth or seventh grader thinking these guys had a pretty good deal. They were out of the war and in a safe place.

I don't think I ever learned whether Robert McLaughlin found the other prisoner the 1978 column says he wanted to look up. I had other people tell me about pleasant memories of contact with POWs who were held at the Florence site.

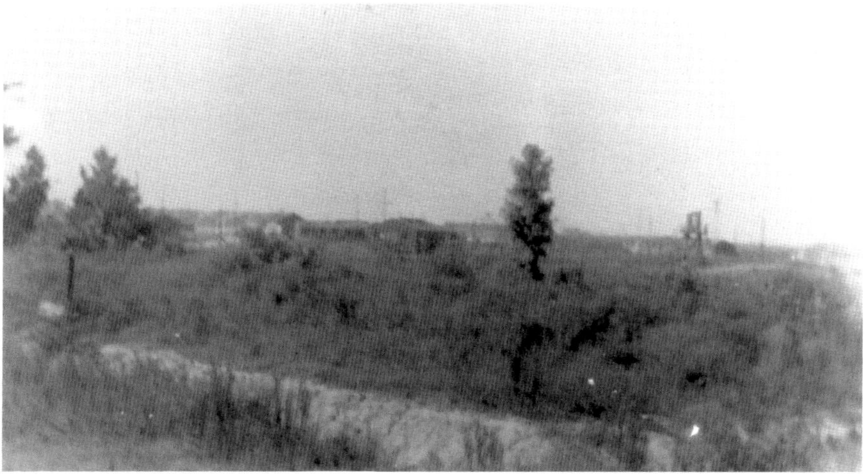

The camp at Florence airport where German POWs were kept late in World War II. *Courtesy of Wayne King.*

There are old stories in town that say that some prisoners sneaked out of the small prison camp at the airport and came into town at nights, and then sneaked back in before daylight.

My mother worked in a civil service job at the air base and spoke well of the POWs. When the war ended and they were shipped back home, one of the prisoners whom she considered particularly nice gave her a framed small ceramic figure as a remembrance, and she was very proud of it. It still hangs in my house. The guy wrote his name and hometown on the back, and I said if I ever got to Germany I would try to look him up like Robert McLaughlin did Hans Mahr. By the time I did get there, the writing on the back of the ceramic figure was unreadable, and it is one of my regrets that I never contacted him.

Shock on a Sunday

Morning News column, December 7, 1981

Forty years ago this morning, Florence people awoke on a Sunday that was one of those mild fall days that we have around here. The sky was mostly clear. It was a little cool but comfortable.

In the *Morning News*, they read that Russian defenders were fighting furiously against German invaders in Moscow suburbs. In the middle pages of the paper, they read that movies were becoming less moral, which obviously was seen as bad, but on a brighter side, a South Carolina college football all-star team had defeated an all-star team from North Carolina, 14–7, in Charlotte.

Mickey Rooney could be seen the next day at the Carolina Theatre in *Life Begins for Andy Hardy*. Jeannette McDonald and Mary Martin also would be in movies the next day. Movies, of course, were not then shown here on Sundays.

A house on Carolina Drive was advertised for sale for $250 down and $29 per month. Super X gasoline was $1.14 for five gallons. Right. Five gallons. Clyburn the Tailor offered a suit for $27.50.

The main front-page story told of President Roosevelt sending a personal message to Emperor Hirohito of Japan asking why Japanese troop concentrations were so great in Indo-China. It was perhaps a last effort to avoid a break with Japan, the story said. And a little paragraph in the regular front-page column called "Did You Ever Stop to Think?"

observed, "Japan is this country's closest bet to war and may yet get us into it. It is evident that the military government of that country is begging us for a fight."

People around town were going home from church later or having Sunday dinner. At the old Hotel Florence, the board of directors of the South Carolina Junior Chamber of Commerce was meeting. The Jaycees board was interrupted. Japanese planes had attacked Pearl Harbor in the Hawaiian Islands, a territorial possession of the United States where our main Pacific naval base was located, and damage was heavy, loss of life great.

The Jaycees from around the state, who had partied and had a dance at the Florence Country Club the night before, sent a telegram to President Roosevelt. They told FDR that the South Carolina Jaycees "in meeting assembled and in full realization of the tremendous effect of Japan's action in shelling Pearl Harbor and our Far Eastern defenses do hereby give our full time to help our country in this emergency."

The files of the *Morning News* do not tell how people by the hundreds, maybe thousands, came into the downtown area late on the day of December 7, 1941. They seemed to find comfort in gathering and walking around, looking rather absent-mindedly at displays in the shop windows, perhaps thinking about Christmas presents, perhaps wondering if Christmas would be the same this year—or ever again.

Lots of them picked up one of the several extra editions that the *Morning News* had put out during the afternoon and evening as more news came in. An inch-and-a-half-high headline on the front of the extras shouted, "Japs Declare War on U.S."

An editorial in the extras said that the United States entered the war its Congress had not declared on the side of the right. "The war is on," the editorial concluded. "Japan fired the first shot. A united America will see to it that Japan does not fire the last shot."

Life went on—and ended. The Monday paper carried several obituaries, and one man died of stabbing wounds.

Radio listeners that night, if they tuned to the right station, heard Paul Covington, son of Dr. and Mrs. D.D. Covington, on *Take It or Leave It* from Chicago.

The *Morning News* office was receiving calls from people in the area who had family members in Hawaii, and Governor J.E. Harley called out the Home Guard to go to the Santee-Cooper hydroelectric plant near Moncks Corner and protect it from possible sabotage. That included a unit from Florence, which went on to serve as an army unit during the war.

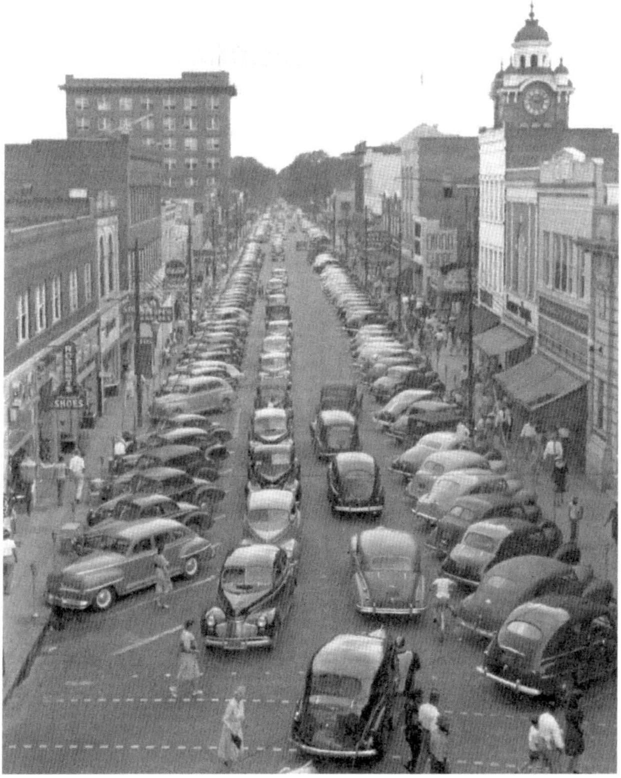

The 100 block of West Evans Street was crowded with shocked people the evening of the Pearl Harbor attack. *Courtesy of Wayne King.*

Landon E. Carter of Florence, state department commander of the Veterans of Foreign Wars, wired Governor Harley that the veterans "stand in readiness to serve their country in any way possible." T.J. Mitchell, county organizer for the aircraft warning sites, called on his people in fifteen aircraft warning sites around the county to get their volunteers ready to man their posts.

Were Florence people angry? Well, the next day the navy recruiting office was open until after midnight because the crowd of volunteers was so great. C.M. Hughes, officer in charge of the navy recruiters, said, "They all seem to want to get at the Japs." The turnout of volunteers, Hughes said, "is just one indication the Japanese didn't know what they were doing when they attacked this country."

The post office and federal building was put under strict security, and identification tags were being issued for people who worked there. Mrs. John L. Bruce called for more contributions for "Bundles for Britain." Judge R.W. Sharkey announced that Florence had a $9,000 goal assigned as part of an emergency $50 million national Red Cross drive. We had, the judge said, "vast and definite responsibilities for services to our armed forces."

While war was at the top of the list of things people were thinking about, Florence never forgot that its main business is business. The December 8 paper carried a photo studio ad offering quick and special attention to people going into the service who wanted photos of themselves.

The State Theatre keyed its ad for a movie to "WAR? You ain't seen anything until you see this girl fight her way into the movies" in its feature attraction.

Big crowds gathered outside Zeigler's Drug Store to look at big pictures that showed the areas in Hawaii that had been hit by the Japanese attack.

Over in Darlington County, governor's officers still were killjoys. They cracked two stills.

The paper was particularly distressed to report that a bomber base that Florence had hoped to land was going to Greenville instead as a result of "political considerations and pressure too difficult to overcome."

On Monday, Peter Jones of Wadesboro, North Carolina, a Confederate veteran, was in town shopping and stated, "Show me Hitler at 100 yards and give me a good gun, and I'll fix him."

Filling station operator Pete Thornell, who expressed opinions in his ads, said in his daily ad, "There are many heartaches ahead and it is wishful thinking to convince ourselves it will be over in a week or two." He got that right. It was late summer of 1945 before the church bells and old steam whistles in the railroad yards sounded to celebrate the end of the war.

2009 Update: Florence felt very involved in World War II, as the railroad played a major part in keeping the war effort going and so many Florence people were involved with the railroad. Wartime scarcity and rationing, as well as service members leaving home, also made the war seem close.

An Army Air Base was established at the Florence Airport, and uniforms were a routine sight on Florence streets during that period.

The end of the war in 1945 brought throngs of people back downtown where they had wandered in uncertainty and confusion on Pearl Harbor Day. But this time there was great joy and relief.

Drive-In Theatres Disappear

Morning News column, November 12, 1980

When the Palmetto Drive-In Theatre closed the other day, it left Florence without a drive-in movie for the first time since just after World War II. I once thought drive-ins were a necessity. I still think they are a necessity.

There once were three drive-in theatres in town that were thriving when movie houses looked like dinosaurs in small towns. At the drive-in, a young couple could bring the whole family at no extra cost and save the cost of a baby-sitter. For those dating, it offered obvious opportunities not available in house theatres.

The first drive-in I can remember here was put up at the old Pee Dee Fairgrounds on the Darlington Highway, just west of Young Pecan Co. A screen was put up beside the Darlington Highway, and cars pulled into a pasture-like area facing the screen. There were big horn speakers atop the screen; there were no in-car speakers. Not having individual speakers caused problems when trains came by across the street. Visitors also couldn't hear when it rained and people put their car windows up. You had to be careful when going to the concession stand not to step in anything left behind by animals from the fair.

A little later, this theatre closed as a new one, named the Ace Drive-In, opened on the Timmonsville Highway near where the old T'ville Highway meets the new one. This new theatre still used horn speakers

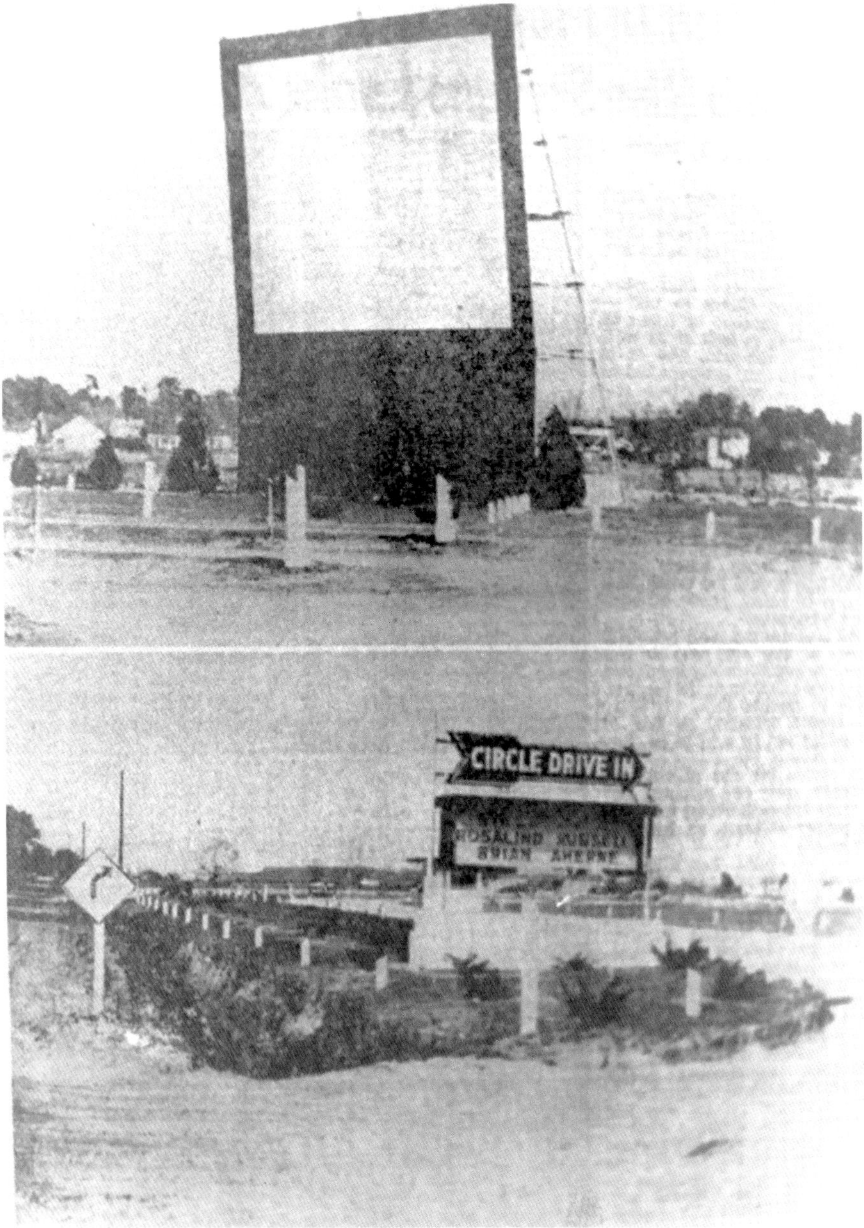

The screen of the Circle Drive-In Theatre in the 1940s, shortly after its opening.

above the screen, but no trains came by. From time to time, this theatre also had adults-only movies on weekends, and we rode bikes all the way out on the Old Timmonsville Highway and sat by a ditch bank to watch for free.

About 1948 or 1949, there was an important development when the Circle Drive-In opened where Kroger now stands. (Vacant in 2009, it was at Evans and Cashua.) This one had the first in-car speakers, and for a time it had a fun land of small carnival rides for the kiddies. It also had playground equipment to lure families out early and do business in the concession stand. The late T.S. Roe, who owned the place, put up small bleachers just in front of the screen with its own speaker for the neighborhood children. Those of us who lived nearby spent a lot of time around the Circle Drive-In, and from time to time made studies of what was going on along the back rows.

Part of the plot we used as a home baseball field for our baseball team, the Cats from Five Points. The dimensions were a little weird: we had a boat pond from the fun land in centerfield, and the right fielder often had to pick his way through speakers to catch fly balls, but it was a great place to play and was rent-free. Who could complain?

The Ace Drive-In added individual speakers, which made it a lot better, and it later took the name of Bright Leaf Drive-In Theater. The last one to open was the Palmetto on the Darlington Highway. This was the theatre that closed down the other day. The screen for the Palmetto was at the back of the plot, facing the highway. This made for problems when standards loosened and more was shown in movies than left to the imagination. When a hot movie played, there was not only a problem of people who were offended seeing the picture from the highway, but also people who were not offended tending to run into one another as they watched.

The Bright Leaf was the first to close, followed by the Circle and then the Palmetto. Maybe they will be back some day.

2009 Update: So far, the drive-in theatres have not reappeared in Florence, and at last count there was only one drive-in theatre operating in the state. The last one in Florence County, just east of Lake City, closed in the 1990s.

A-Bomb Spotlights Mars Bluff

"We still get calls asking us about it," said Walter Gregg of the life-changing experience he and his Mars Bluff area family had on March 11, 1958. They were minding their own business, working or playing, when a terrific explosion rocked everything. It stripped the trees around their house of foliage, left a big crater about one hundred yards from their house and damaged their home beyond repair.

"I thought at first a plane had crashed," said Gregg, then a conductor for the Atlantic Coast Line Railroad. He had just heard airplanes passing.

A little later, they realized that the U.S. Air Force had accidentally dropped an atomic bomb on their property. Fortunately, it was not armed to explode as a nuclear weapon, but the TNT designed to trigger a nuclear explosion caused quite a bit of damage and created an international news story.

The Greggs' three children—nine-year-old Frances and six-year-old twins Walter Jr. and Helen—and cousin Ella Davies were playing in the yard, Mrs. Gregg was sewing in the house and Mr. Gregg was working outside when the explosion occurred. Half an hour earlier, the children had been about where the bomb fell. The story then would have been tragic.

Mrs. Gregg, stunned and bleeding from a cut on her head, made her way through the wrecked house. Mr. Gregg was stunned but quickly recovered and came to check on her. The children were knocked to the ground, but only one had a cut that required stitches.

Teenagers Guy Moore and Russell Culberson were driving toward town on Highway 76/301, a couple of hundred yards away, when the concussion

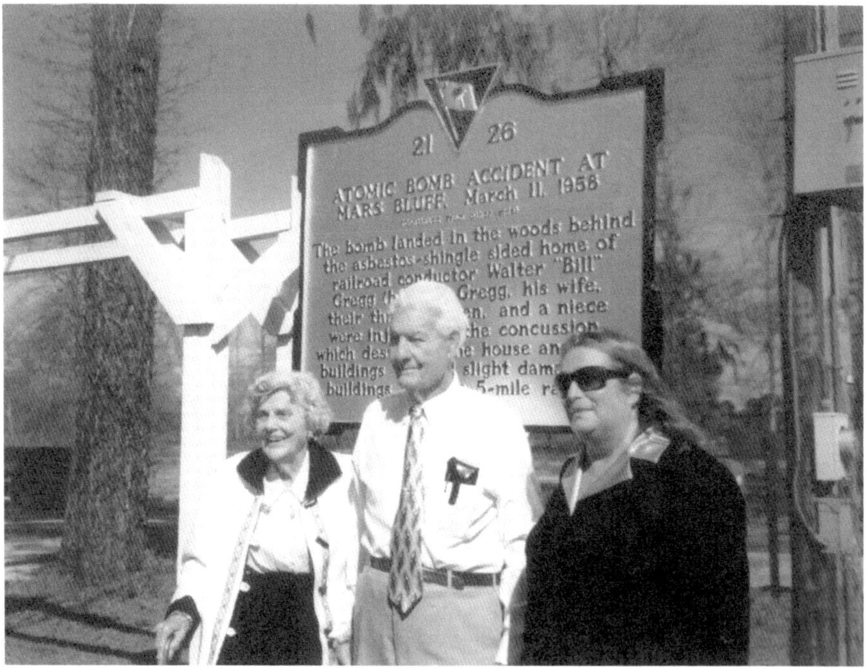

Mr. and Mrs. Walter Gregg at the 2009 unveiling of the historical marker about the atomic bomb accident. Marshall Yarborough of the Florence Historical Commission is at right.

nearly knocked them off the road. They investigated and found the Gregg family hurt and stunned at their ruined home. They took the Greggs to McLeod Infirmary, where they were treated and released, except for Ella Davies, who had numerous stitches and was kept overnight.

A wide area was shaken by the concussion, and many heard the blast. Cracked plaster and windows were reported. At the Mispah Baptist Church about a quarter-mile away, windows were broken, glass was scattered and pews were knocked around by the blast. The pulpit Bible was thrown to the floor.

The plane from Hunter Air Force Base near Savannah was flying a training mission with a big, ten-foot-long atomic bomb that was not armed as a nuclear weapon. Had it been armed, it would have had about twice the strength of the Hiroshima atomic bomb of World War II, the Air Force said.

Later, it was learned that a pin that secured the bomb aboard the B-47 seemed to be malfunctioning because a warning light came on. As a crew member tried to fix it, the plane shuddered and the bomb fell onto the bomb bay doors and then broke through. The crewman nearly fell from the plane. He informed the cockpit that they had accidentally dropped their bomb. They radioed the news and headed back to Savannah.

The big bomb fell into soft, muddy soil about one hundred yards from the Greggs' house, creating a crater about fifty feet across and thirty-five feet deep. The crater is still there and usually holds several feet of water. It was explained that the softness of the soil softened the explosion and perhaps avoided fatalities, as the bomb sank somewhat into the earth before exploding. If the ground had been harder, they say, it would have been much worse.

The Air Force reacted quickly. They secured the area and inspected the damage. Some reserve members were on hand before that, joined by local law officers, including the highway patrol.

It was a big news story. *Morning News* staffers fielded phone calls from newspapers and broadcasters around the country and overseas who were seeking local details. It became an international incident, and many people were upset to learn that Air Force planes flew over the United States carrying nuclear weapons.

Air Force representatives met with Florence mayor David H. McLeod and other community leaders to express regret and explain the importance

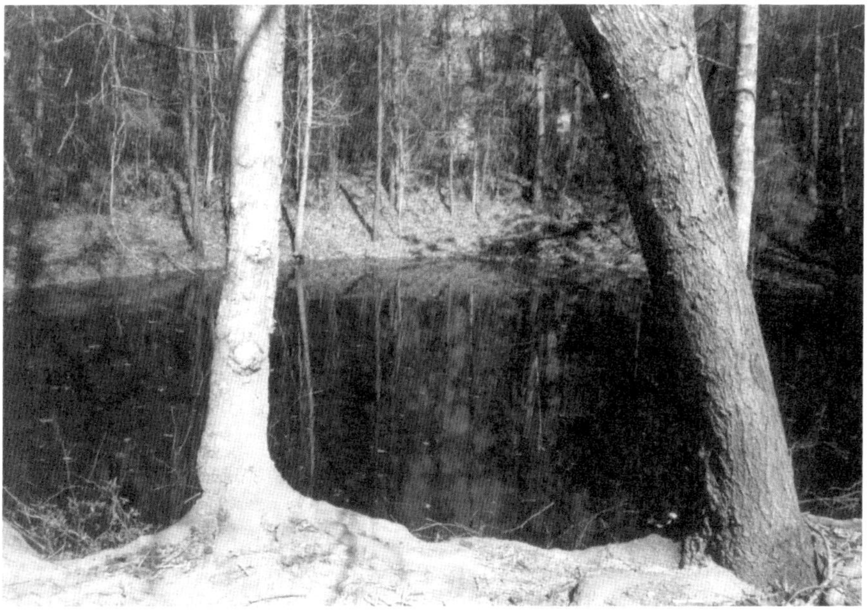

The crater made by the atomic bomb is still there but was nearly filled with water in early 2009.

of Air Force capability and training at the height of the Cold War. McLeod said that the Florence community understood the importance of national defense and the need for military training.

Quick and careful checks determined that there was no danger from radiation, but the Greggs were restricted in visits back to their wrecked house. Mrs. Gregg said that they were not permitted to take much out, but vandals got in and took money and jewelry. "They knew the difference between costume jewelry and more valuable jewelry," she said, "and they left the costume jewelry."

The Greggs got what was considered small compensation from the government, even after a court case. They moved into Florence, and the house, damaged beyond repair, was destroyed.

It all faded into the background, except for occasional writers who contacted the Greggs while working on stories. However, Gregg said that all of the B-47 crew eventually visited them, apologizing for the incident.

On March 11, 2008, the Florence County Historical Commission staged a fiftieth anniversary commemoration with a ceremony beside the crater. After speeches were given, the crowd viewed a film about the incident in the fellowship hall of the Mispah Church, which was damaged by the bomb explosion. The fellowship hall actually was the church in 1958, but a new sanctuary was built since then and the old sanctuary moved to serve in its new role.

A year later, on March 8, 2009, in a ceremony beside nearby Highway 76/301, a historical marker briefly telling the story of the incident was unveiled. Mr. and Mrs. Gregg unveiled the marker.

Florence's Wayward Santa

Morning News column, December 22, 2002

This event took place something like forty years ago and was one of the most extraordinary moments in *Morning News* history. We won't use names here, but in the early 1960s, there was a young Florence schoolteacher who did odd reporting jobs at the paper during school vacations. A Florence store staged an unusual stunt that holiday season: Santa Claus was to jump from an airplane and land in the store parking lot one evening and then enter the store to listen to demands from children.

It's exciting for kids to see Santa Claus in person; to sit on Santa's knee and tell him firsthand what they would like for him to come down their chimney with a bound and leave under their tree is greater. Throw in watching him come from an airplane by parachute, and you have a formula that excites parents as well. Many area people turned out to see this, and we thought that it would be a good idea to cover it, since it had about the biggest crowd in town that night. The young teacher got the assignment.

The reporter appeared at the thronged parking lot and watched the airplane carrying Santa pass high overhead. People watched expectantly. Finally, Santa jumped, carrying a flare so the crowd could watch his descent. It quickly became clear that someone had not accurately calculated the winds. Santa drifted farther and farther from the parking lot. He would land nowhere near the store.

Our young reporter thought, quite correctly, that it would be good for him to go find Santa and get quotes on this strange experience. He drove

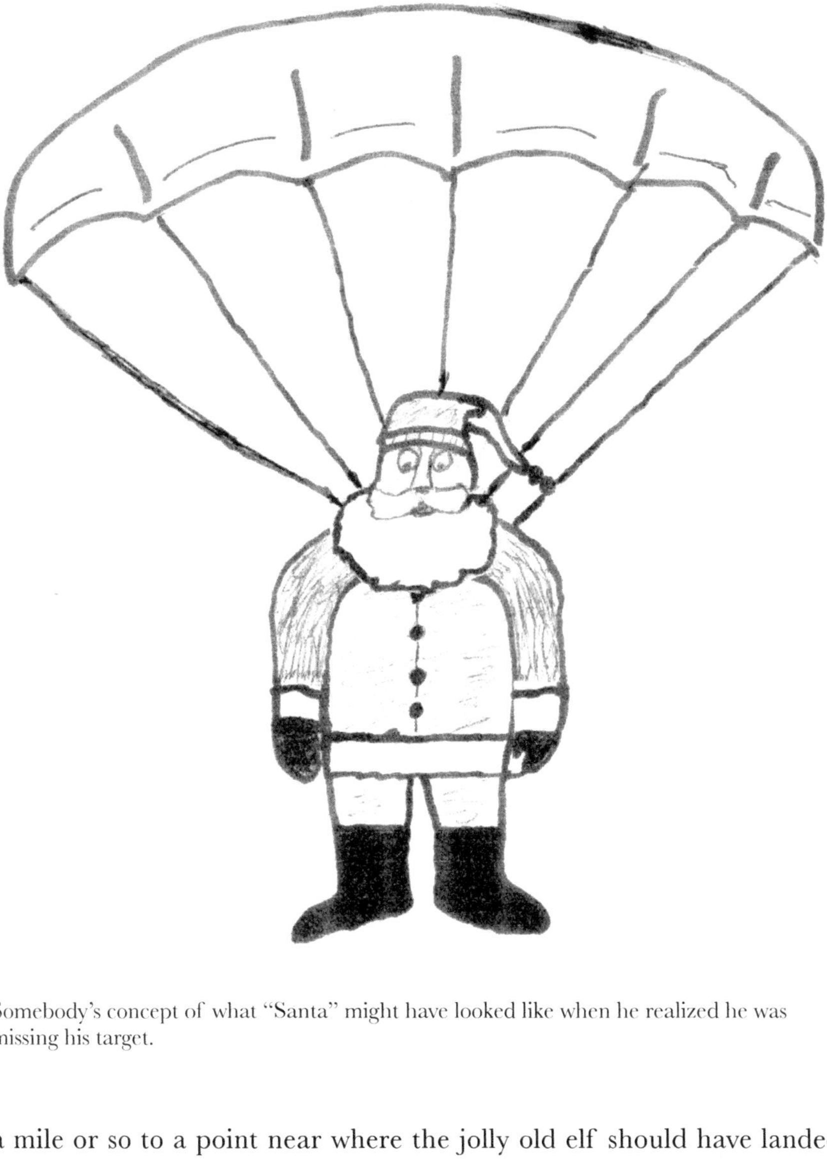

Somebody's concept of what "Santa" might have looked like when he realized he was missing his target.

a mile or so to a point near where the jolly old elf should have landed, got out of his car and went into the woods calling for Santa.

Then the reporter realized that not only was he not finding Santa Claus, but he also had no idea where his car was. He was lost. He trudged through the woods and then spotted a light in the distance. Making his way toward it, he broke into a small clearing around an isolated house. *Maybe they will let me use a phone*, he thought, *to call the office, tell them what happened and figure out a way to get back to the car.*

He crossed the little clearing and stepped onto the back porch so he could knock on the door. Then a woman stepped out of the shower just inside a window beside the porch. Stunned, he froze momentarily as she spotted him only about ten feet or so away and emitted a blood-curdling scream. He remained frozen long enough for a big Hulk Hoganesque husband to burst onto the porch and back our unfortunate reporter against the wall. The husband demanded to know what our young representative was doing peeping at his wife.

"That's not it," the reporter told him. "I was lost and hoping I could use your phone."

So what, the husband reasonably inquired, was he doing walking around these thick woods at this time of night? All the reporter could think to do was tell him the plain truth. "I was looking for Santa Claus."

Well, you can imagine. As the outraged husband prepared to beat him into next week, our unfortunate reporter desperately explained that Santa mistakenly had come down by parachute somewhere nearby and he (the reporter) was just looking for him. That was all.

Just as our husband prepared to give our reporter a painful lesson, both heard a sound nearby. They turned, and what to the wondering eyes of the husband and the reporter should appear, but Santa Claus walking out of the woods and across the backyard, carrying a parachute.

It was a little like a New York editor's answer to a little girl's question. Yes (fill in the blank), there is a Santa Claus. So the husband, still not entirely happy about the whole thing, realized that it was all an unfortunate mistake and let them use the telephone. I'm not sure about this part, but I think the husband gave them a lift back to the reporter's car and the store.

So have a nice Christmas, but I doubt that Santa will bring any of you a nicer present than he brought that young reporter just by emerging from the woods that night and saving him from an outraged husband.

I know. I know. You think I'm putting you on, but I swear this is the truth. Oh, the teacher left town long ago, but not because of this.

Nice Christmas Present

Shortly before Thanksgiving 1965, Mr. and Mrs. Arthur Braveboy, who lived near Coward, got the sad news that fifty-eight thousand American families received during the Vietnam War. Their twenty-four-year-old son, Toby, had died in action, a telegram said. The Defense Department asked where to ship the body. The *Morning News* carried an obituary on the young man.

Then came thrilling new information. Mrs. Valerie Durant, who ran the Lake City Western Union office, described it. Mrs. Durant had delivered the sad news the previous Monday. "I get as upset as the families," she said of such messages. "So far I have been able to locate someone close to the families to help me make deliveries."

Two days after sharing the sad news with the Braveboy family, she was stunned by another message that she received for the Braveboys: their son had been found alive and was in a field hospital. He was wounded, but the outlook was good.

"I gummed it down and cried," Mrs. Durant said of the Defense Department telegram that reported that Braveboy had been found. She sped to the Braveboy home, believing that if the highway patrol stopped her for speeding they would have given her an escort.

Like the earlier telegram, it changed things. When the first telegram arrived, Mrs. Braveboy had cancelled family Thanksgiving plans. Now, she said, the holiday was back on. Thanksgiving was the next day, but she promised all the trimmings.

"I'm just sorry that Toby is not here now," she said of the Thanksgiving observance, but knowing that he would be returning home later made it her best Thanksgiving.

Mrs. Durant's deliveries had really changed things in that household. On Monday, Mrs. Braveboy had been packing a box to ship to Toby. He wanted a package with "lots of junk, especially candy." As she packed "candy, chewing gum, cookies and fruit cake, razor blades and a wrist watch the family had bought to replace one he had lost," she needed a bigger box. Her husband went into Lake City to get one.

While he was gone, the first telegram arrived, saying that Toby had died. On Tuesday, another telegram inquired where the body should be shipped. On Wednesday came the thrilling news that he was safe.

There was a big family gathering that Thanksgiving. PFC Toby Braveboy was not physically present, but he was the main thing on everybody's mind. While his family celebrated that Thanksgiving, the young soldier was in an army hospital. But on Christmas Eve, he pulled up in his parents' yard. What a celebration this Christmas saw! His grandmother, Mrs. Willie Evans, said, "I'm eighty-one years old and this is the best Christmas I've ever had."

Toby had been moved from a field hospital in Vietnam to the Philippines, and then to the big army hospital at Fort Sam Houston, Texas, and finally to Fort Benning, Georgia. He was to spend about two more weeks at the Benning institution for surgery on shrapnel wounds in his legs.

"It's sure my best Christmas," he said. He had lost twenty-five to thirty pounds during the ordeal but was gaining weight and strength. He got lots of attention as neighboring children gathered to hear his stories.

His unit had been on patrol near Pleiku when they were overwhelmed by a much bigger force of Viet Cong. Of his eleven-man squad, only Braveboy survived. When the Viet Cong overran the area, Braveboy was wounded and lying in tall grass. He played dead as the VC looked around. One U.S. soldier was decapitated.

A young VC noticed that Braveboy was still alive and raised his rifle to shoot him. "I held up my wounded hand to him, and he lowered his rifle and walked away," Braveboy said. "Maybe he just thought I would die anyway and wanted to save ammunition."

After they left, it was a week before Braveboy was spotted by a U.S. helicopter. "When the helicopter got up, I felt good, real good, in spite of my wounds. I knew I was going to be all right."

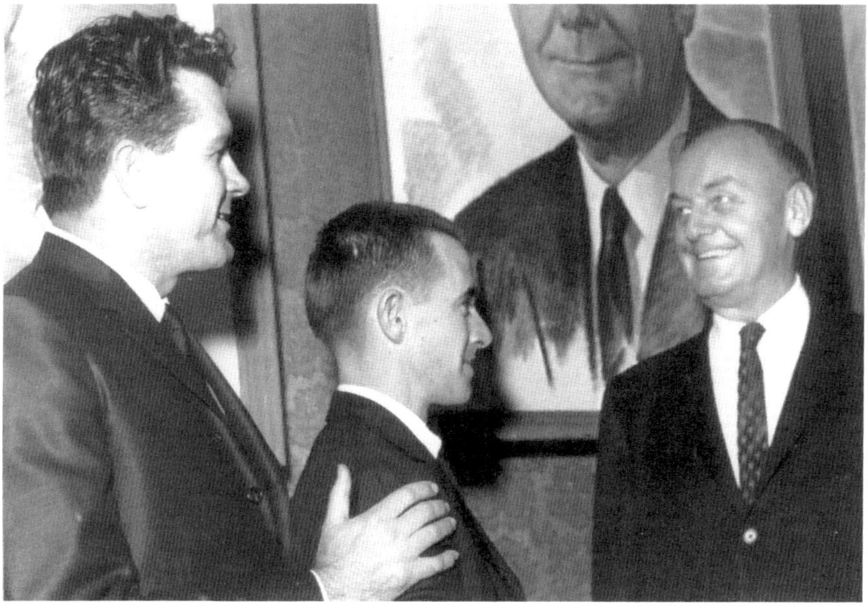

Toby Braveboy (center) gets honors in Columbia. At left is Congressman Albert Watson. *Courtesy of Pansy B. Baker.*

Fried chicken being his favorite, his mother said that a big platter awaited him, and he had more than one hundred letters and Christmas cards to read from all over the country. Much more mail was to arrive.

The Christmas Day celebration was for family, but a reunion at the community center followed with many more people expected. The entire area was thrilled at the Braveboys' good fortune, and pictures of the parents and Toby ran in newspapers all over the country. *ABC News* sent them a tape of Braveboy's segment on their evening news, and Walter Cronkite signed off the *CBS Evening News*, remarking on the irony that "Braveboy was from Coward."

The postscript is not as uplifting as the story above. Toby Braveboy came home from the army and settled back into civilian life, but a few years later, he was in a wreck on a Florence County road. He died at age thirty.

Snowfall of 1973

Old-timers tell about hurricanes in Florence, including Hazel and Hugo, but this is an area where occasional hurricanes can be expected.

Florence was shaken and numerous stories were told, but not much damage came from the 1886 Charleston earthquake. But we are near a fault where occasional tremors can be expected.

Tornadoes have hit, including one in 1924 that swept across the county, causing death and destruction. Again, some twisters can be expected.

But enough snow to stop Buffalo is not something you expect in this very southern area. That's what makes the snowfall of 1973 so unusual in Florence weather history.

On February 9, 1973, the forecast was for partly cloudy and cold with a high near forty degrees. It was opening night at Florence Little Theatre. Snow started to fall just before show time and covered the roads when the audience headed home.

The next morning, a Saturday for which fair weather was predicted, snow still fell heavily, a serious problem for drivers little experienced with the slippery stuff. Many businesses did not open, and most that did closed early as the snow continued.

It finally stopped that night after about twenty-four hours of heavy snowfall, and the official measurement at the airport weather station was seventeen inches. It fell statewide, but from Orangeburg along I-95 to Florence saw the heaviest snowfall. Orangeburg had twenty-one inches.

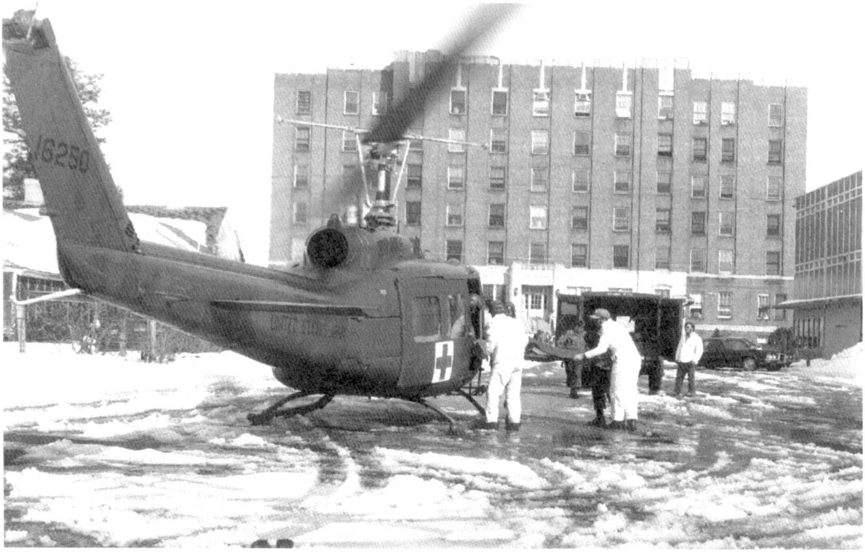

A Cheves Street parking lot served as a makeshift heliport to transport patients to McLeod Memorial Hospital in the background.

By Saturday afternoon, nearly everything was stopped. An example was the *Morning News*, which was unable to assemble a workforce. If it had had enough workers to produce a paper, it could not have been delivered. The edition was cancelled, probably the only scheduled day of publication the paper has missed in nearly ninety years.

Drifts measured by the feet on many streets, stopping traffic. Helicopters transported hospital patients. I-95 was closed, and the military helped get stranded motorists to safety. Motels along the interstate were jammed with stranded people, and armories and schools became emergency shelters. It was estimated on Sunday that about one thousand motorists were stranded on county highways. Thirteen reportedly walked off Highway 301 to the DuPont plant near Florence and spent the night. Some spent the night in their cars.

A soldier going home for the first time in two years spent a third of his leave stuck in Florence.

Although there was much discomfort and inconvenience, only four South Carolina deaths were reported, none in Florence County.

By Tuesday, thawing had begun in earnest, and stranded people were getting back on roads, with traffic heavy and slow and much starting and stopping. A New Jersey man stranded at a Florence motel received army

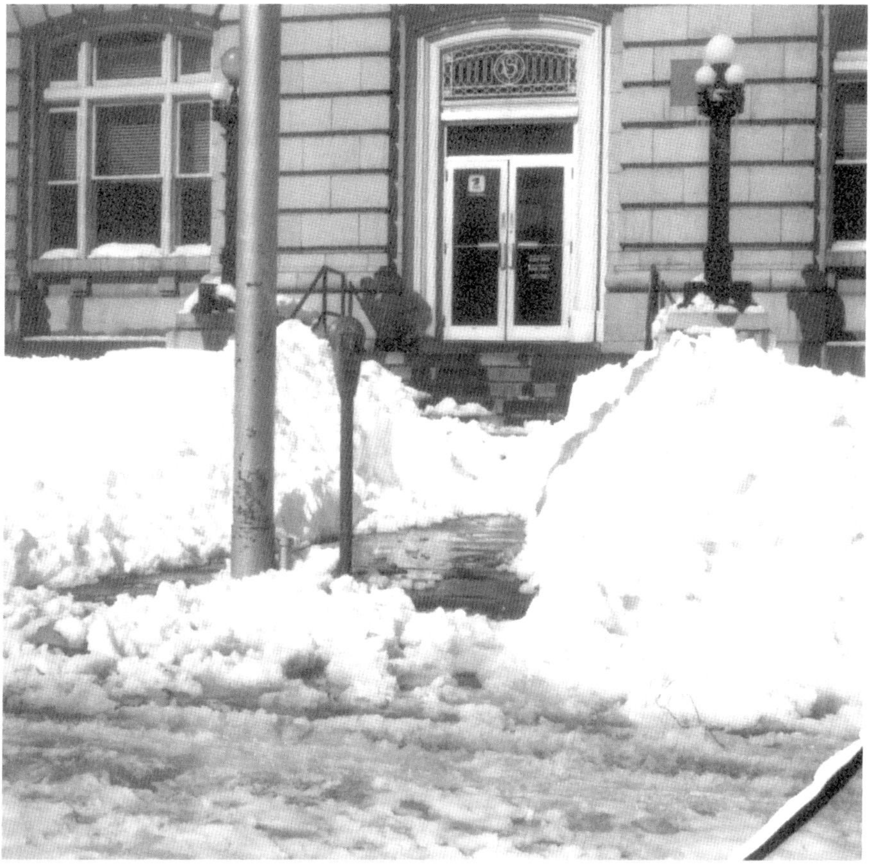

Several-foot-high snowdrifts pile up beside the old Florence Post Office steps as a result of the big snowstorm of 1973.

food, which he said was no better than in 1944, but he was glad to get it. One Massachusetts woman, frustrated over lack of equipment to deal with such a storm, said that she was writing the governor to complain, and asked, "What is the name of the mayor of this town?"

A New York woman said that her party was helped out of an ice jam and made it to a motel, where they stayed for three days. "Everybody wanted to do all they could for us, and the other travelers pitched in, too," she said. At the hotel where she was stranded, she said that people slept in halls, the dining room and the lobby while food arrived by helicopter.

A Florence motel manager said that in the kitchen of his motel one night he saw almost nobody he knew. 'The visitors had just pitched in to help feed each other." Some had food service experience and put it to good use. He said most were nice but one angry woman wore out his patience. "I finally just told her it was an act of God and suggested that she talk to Him about it."

The driver of one car with New Jersey tags described the hardships, but a little girl in the back seat said, "I wish it would happen again. It was lots of fun." This comment drew cold stares from the adults.

By Wednesday, the temperature had increased enough to let traffic approach normal, and the shelters were cleared.

Businesses and schools were closed for several days. For local people, there was inconvenience but not the hardship that travelers had. Utilities mostly held up, and when the thaw came, Florence County went back to work. Emergency personnel talked about being better prepared if such a storm hit again, but not many expected anything like it anytime soon. It has not happened again as we near the end of the first decade of the twenty-first century.

Moving Day for McLeod

Morning News column, November 16, 1979

The *Morning News* called it "marvelous in its conception and in its execution and in its wonderful equipment. Nothing has been omitted in the construction of the most modern hospital of the present day." The night after dedication ceremonies, it was reported that "those who visited the handsome structure last night were attracted by the beautiful sight it presented from the exterior with lights blazing from every window for every one of the seven floors."

The Reverend W.S. Poynor, longtime rector of St. John's Episcopal Church, was the main speaker at the February 20, 1935 dedication, and he said, "The people of Florence have every reason to rejoice and be glad because of this great and magnificent Infirmary and its founder, Dr. [Frank H.] McLeod, and to lift up their hearts and voices and give thanks to God for the gift of this wonderful institution."

Last night, nearly forty-five years later, patients spent their last night in the McLeod Infirmary, which a few years ago was renamed McLeod Memorial Hospital. If things go as planned today, by nightfall all of the patients will be housed four blocks east on Cheves Street in the new McLeod Regional Medical Center. The old building will stand dark and lonely, having in its later years been called dated, dirty and inadequate, a far cry from the proud remarks Florentines made about it in the first half of its service to the area. The $30 million new hospital will have luxuries and services not available in its predecessor and treatments and hope not available anywhere in 1935.

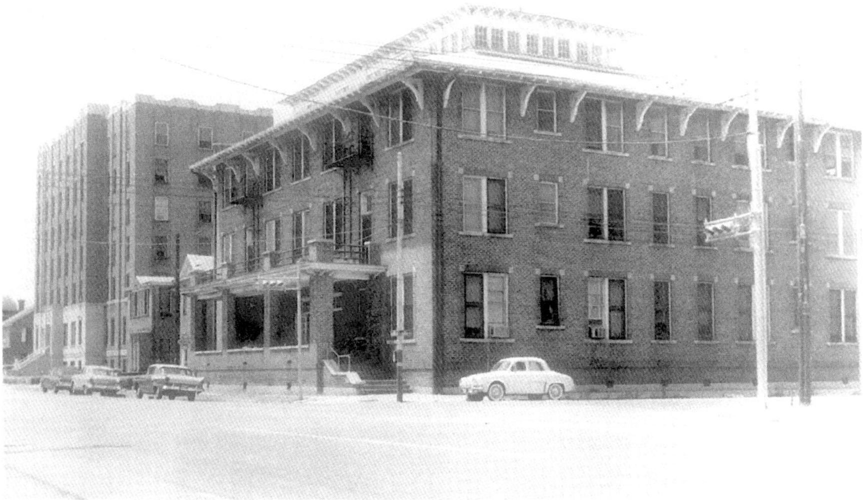

The hospital was abandoned when McLeod moved. The main building is at left; the nurses' dorm, which was previously the main hospital building, is at right. *Courtesy of McLeod Regional Medical Center.*

Anybody who has lived in Florence all of his life has to have some memories of the building we are nearly finished with. If the older people in my family had realized how delighted I was when one of them was in McLeod's when I was a kid, I probably would not be here writing this now. But when a relative landed there, and several of them did, it gave me the run of the place if I stayed fairly quiet and didn't let the doctors know how much I was running about. I could accompany a visiting party and spend time on the elevators, watch comings and goings through what then was a much bigger and more luxurious lobby and, best of all, look out at the town from the upper floors.

I didn't care much for the southern view. It was mostly residential area and trees. But looking out the back of the building gave a great view of the downtown business area when there truly was one, and the view toward the east was of the railroad yards when they really were busy. During World War II, trains waited to get into town. It is a miracle that auto traffic moved at all, the street crossings were blocked so often with trains hauling war materiel and personnel.

I usually could look out of the sixth-floor windows all I wanted, but I had to tread lightly on the seventh (top) floor because the operating rooms were up there, and it was not a place they needed kids fooling around. Still, I eased up there as often as I could to gaze through the east windows down at the three-story nurses' home on the corner of Cheves and Dargan to see if it really was true that you could peer through a skylight to see nurses sunbathing in the nude. Maybe it was true, but I never caught them at it.

I had quite a crush on a student nurse once. She looked great in her student nurse's uniform that featured a sort of blue-gray blouse and a white and blue cap. Whenever I got to go to McLeod's, I quickly found out what was her shift, and she was very nice to me. But one day I came in and she had finished her training. Now she was dressed in a full white nurse's uniform. I was crushed and never did like her as much again. She was cuter in the other uniform. Women are fickle, I decided.

Then there was the elevator operator I liked and got on with well. I rode many vertical miles with her, and she let me handle opening the grill-like gate that separated the passengers in the car from the outer doors on each floor. One night I finally talked her into letting me run the contraption, and I got off to a good start, but I didn't understand that the handle you started it with had to be held in place. Once we were moving good, I let it go and we came to a sudden halt that probably just missed putting McLeod's in the market for a new elevator. That ended my elevator-operating career.

When I was about seven, I got to be a patient, and I figured this would be an adventure. It was. As I went under the ether for a tonsillectomy, huge spiders and ants and slimy creatures and multicolored octopuses and things like that were messing with me. When I awoke in my room, I had thrown up and worse all over myself, and my throat hurt up a storm.

I began to wonder about Dr. M.R. Mobley, who had seemed so kindly in the preoperative visits. He had all kinds of sticks and sprays and a coated brush he mopped out my throat with before it was all over. Dr. Mobley was the Ayatollah Khomeini of my seventh year. I steered clear of him in the future, and it must have been twenty-five years or so later when I saw him next. He told me who he was, and I told him who I was and that he had removed my tonsils.

"Well, I'm sorry," he said, "I don't remember."

"Don't worry," I told him. "I remember well enough for both of us," and he seemed to like that.

My time around that hospital was a little like my short career operating the elevator. It had its ups and downs. My mother and a grandmother died there, but my sons were born there, and it seems like more years than not one or the other of them has been back for renovations.

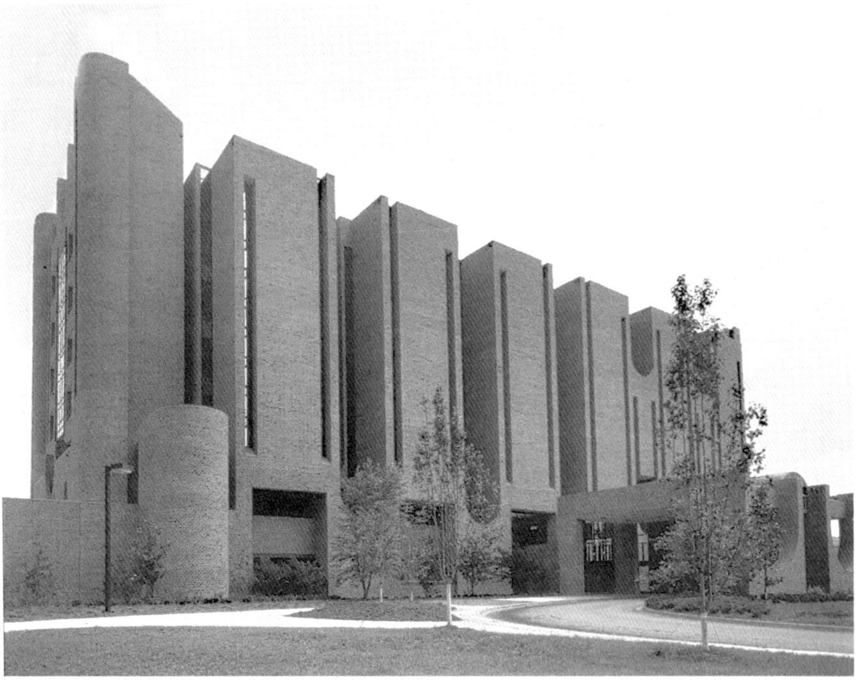

The main building of the McLeod Regional Medical Center, into which the hospital moved in 1979. The campus has about a dozen buildings in 2009. *Courtesy of McLeod Regional Medical Center.*

I was waiting outside in a car while my mother visited a sick friend at McLeod's in the spring of 1945 when I heard on the radio that President Roosevelt had died. Years later, I pulled several days of army basic training as a patient there with a mild case of pneumonia. Dr. Harry Allen had the good sense to put me in McLeod's rather than send me to Fort Jackson by ambulance.

And some years later, I followed Winnie the Pooh through the children's floor.

I'm told that my first trips there were in parents' arms to watch excavation for the foundation. I don't remember that, but I do know that the main hospital was at the corner of Cheves and Dargan when I was born and the building they are now vacating was then only a gleam in Dr. Frank McLeod's eye.

I'm a couple of years older than that building, and I'll appreciate it if you'll stop talking about how old and worn out it is.

2009 Update: The move anticipated in that 1979 column went smoothly, and that night the old building was vacant. I went inside that night and found it dark, lonely and really a little spooky.

In the 1990s, the old hospital was torn down when no use for it was developed. A little earlier, the nurses' home on the corner of Cheves and Dargan also was torn down after a fire. It was sad in both cases. Now all of the old McLeod buildings are gone, replaced by a large vacant lot in the middle of the downtown.

There must be a dozen buildings on the new campus a few blocks east, and it includes a twelve-story tower. McLeod Regional Medical Center is now the county's largest employer.

Lost Florence

When veteran Florentines talk about how things used to be, they likely will talk about things that have disappeared. More than half of the downtown business district has disappeared. Several blocks went at once in the name of urban renewal, but for years after that destruction, little more than weeds materialized there, though some of the space is occupied in 2009. So much was leveled for urban renewal that one is reminded of the American in Vietnam who said, "We had to destroy the village in order to save it."

One building comes to mind when old-timers think of lost Florence: the old city hall on the 100 block of West Evans. It had complicated Gothic architecture and a dramatic several-stories-high clock tower with faces on all four sides. It is said that sometimes all four clock faces reported the same time. Once a Florence youth got in big trouble for shattering one of the clock faces with a rifle.

The building was about twenty feet from the sidewalk. Besides city offices, it also contained the Opera House, which saw little opera but became the Colonial Theatre, a movie house. A marquee later flew from the door to the sidewalk. By the 1930s, fishponds flanked the entrance walkway. Sculptures of frogs squirted water into the ponds and big goldfish swam among lily pads. Mischievous children sometimes tried to catch the goldfish.

About 1950, the most terrifying words to be heard in Florence were uttered: "We're going to modernize." They extended the city hall's front walls to the sidewalk, stripped away the trimmings and decapitated the clock tower. They covered the front with some stucco-like stuff. It added city office

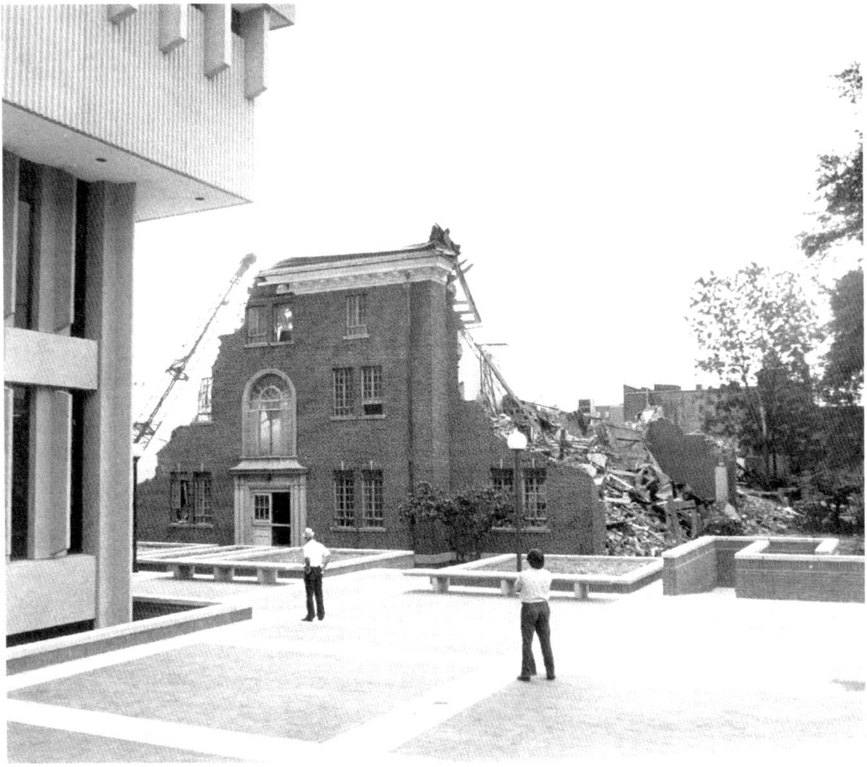

The old Florence County Courthouse being torn down after the Florence City-County Complex opened in 1972. *Courtesy of Sonny Smith.*

space but eliminated the fishponds and stole the structure's personality. Nobody knows what happened to the evicted goldfish.

Finally, in the 1970s, when the City-County Complex was built to house the city and county, what was left of the old city hall was improved into eighteen parking places. There was little protest since the building was nothing to look at after "modernization."

The City-County Complex and hunger for parking cost us another memorable building: the old Florence County Courthouse on the 100 block of North Irby. The old courthouse was built in the early 1890s just after Florence became the county seat. It first looked much like a church with a tower and ornate architecture. In the 1930s, the WPA enlarged and renovated it.

The tower disappeared, but the result was not bad. The building faced Irby with big, dramatic windows to the second-floor courtroom. There was a nice little courthouse ground of maybe sixty feet between the sidewalk and the big porch that stretched across much of the front. As the city hall was razed, so was the old courthouse. It became about thirty parking places.

Probably the biggest destroyed building in the downtown was the 1935 McLeod Infirmary on the 100 block of West Cheves Street. It was impressive when new, seven stories tall, tied with the Trust Building for tallest in town. An unfortunate rear wing was added in the 1950s, but from the front it looked fine. After the infirmary evolved into McLeod Regional Medical Center, it moved down Cheves Street and the 1935 building was left vacant. Various proposals were floated for its use, but none worked. In the 1990s, it was razed.

A little earlier, a three-story building at the corner of Dargan and Cheves that once had been the hospital was lost. It went up about the mid-teens, and after the 1935 building became the hospital, it became quarters for nurses, popularly known as the nurses' home. It was a nice-looking structure with an impressive porch across the front. Vagrants apparently slept there while it was vacant, and finally a fire damaged the building. Many hoped that it would be saved, but it was torn down. Both of those old McLeod buildings had character, but the space they occupied is a plot of grass in 2009.

A few blocks down Dargan Street from the old downtown was Saunders Memorial Hospital, which had three stories and sort of an Old South character with a big porch and a stairway to a second-floor entrance. It became Florence General Hospital, which built a seven-story building on the Irby Street end of the property.

Both were imposing buildings and are now gone, but at least the handsome Drs. Bruce and Lee Foundation Library now occupies the space. Florence General became part of Carolinas Hospital System after a merger with Bruce Hospital.

On the 100 block of East Evans there were great losses. The old Sanborn Hotel was once the Central Hotel and a link to the history of Florence. It was one of the oldest buildings on the block, and across the street was the Hotel Florence. Built about 1908, the four-story Hotel Florence probably was the tallest building in town before the seven-story Trust Building went up during World War I. The hotel was a stylish old building with a second-story balcony overlooking the street and a series of arches along the sidewalk. Go through the arches, and you were on a comfortable verandah a couple of steps up from the sidewalk.

One day the dreaded "We're going to modernize" was uttered, and the hotel's brick and stone front was covered with shiny, plastic-looking facing used on many storefronts during the 1950s. The balcony came down, the

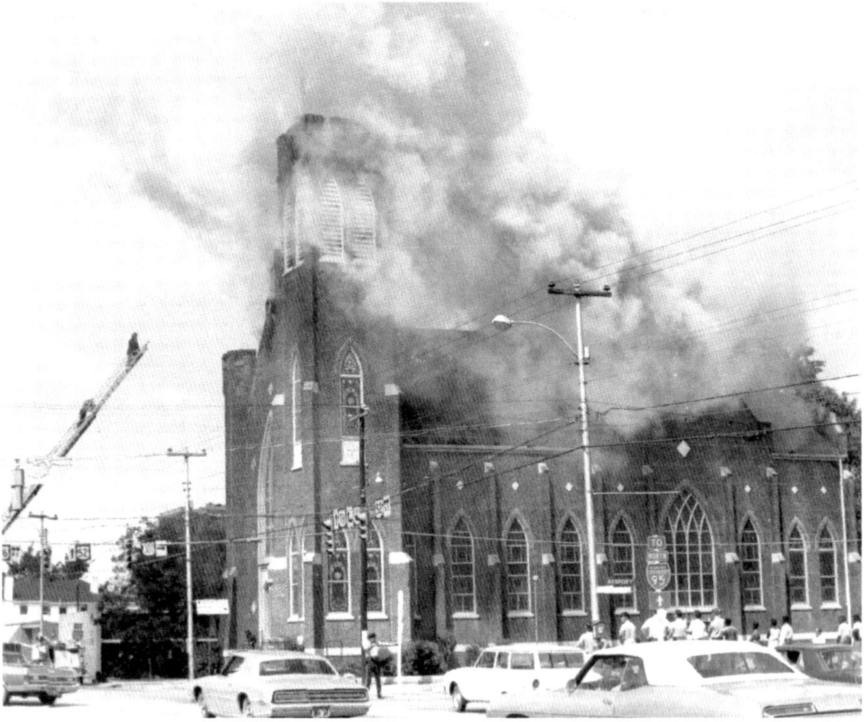

St. Anthony Catholic Church during the 1970s fire that destroyed it. The church moved to the outskirts of town in a new building. *Courtesy of Sonny Smith.*

arches were closed and the verandah was taken into the building. After that, it probably was merciful when it was razed years later.

The old First Presbyterian Church was on that block, set back from the sidewalk with columns across the front. It was a handsome building that was abandoned about 1950 and, after demolition, of course, became parking places.

The 100 block of East Evans was probably the most exciting in town, a real urban block. It is all gone.

Beside the tracks where Ravenel Street dead-ends, the old YMCA stood. It was another big building for a town like Florence. It went up before 1920 with a gymnasium and such on the ground floor and two floors above that with a meeting hall, offices and transients' rooms. An outdoor stairway led to a building-wide second-floor porch and the main entrance. Many local meetings were held there, and at one time most of the city recreation department indoor activities were there. It was demolished in the 1960s.

Downtown churches razed besides First Presbyterian included First Baptist, St. Anthony Catholic Church, Immanuel Baptist and Cumberland United Methodist Church.

St. Anthony was badly damaged by fire and abandoned for a Hoffmeyer Road site, and Cumberland is being rebuilt much as it was. Both were impressive old buildings. The Presbyterian Church and Immanuel moved to Cherokee Road, and First Baptist built a new sanctuary next door before taking its 1890s church down.

Florence's most impressive nineteenth-century school building housed Florence High School on the 100 block of East Cheves until 1921. It was torn down about 1939. The auto agencies replacing it have been razed, and the property is part of the parking lot for the Department of Health and Environmental Control district office.

Not all that has been lost were buildings. Once, an ACL switching tower was at the Evans Street railroad crossing, a frame structure from

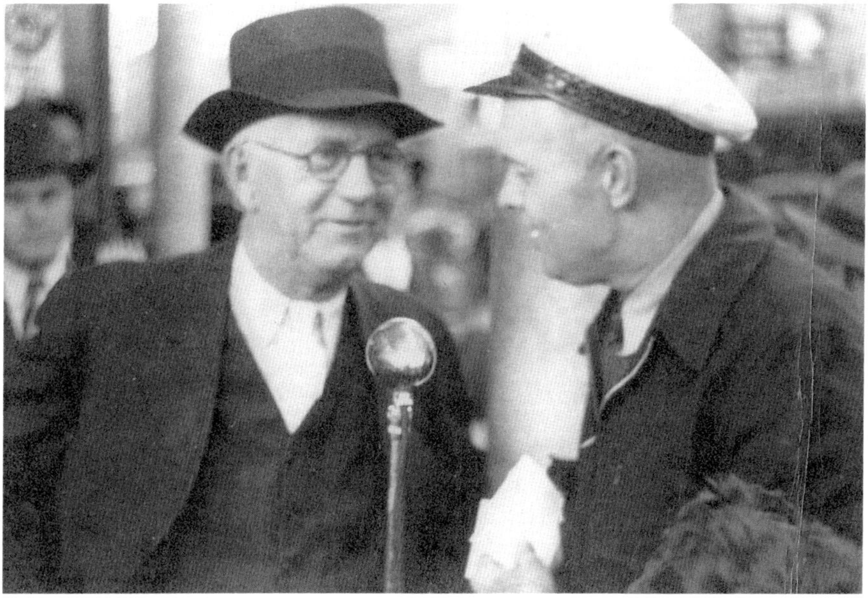

Pete Thornell, a Florence businessman, had a man-on-the-street WOLS radio show, in which he conducted interviews and awarded prizes at the corner of Evans and Dargan Streets, attracting lunchtime crowds. Here, Thornell (right) interviews guest A.P. Chambliss of Pee Dee. Thornell also ran a small chain of Super X low-price gasoline stations and the city bus line, among other enterprises. During World War II, he published a small mimeographed *Bus News* on Mondays when the *Morning News* suspended Monday publication as a wartime conservation measure. *Courtesy of Isabelle C. Clemmons.*

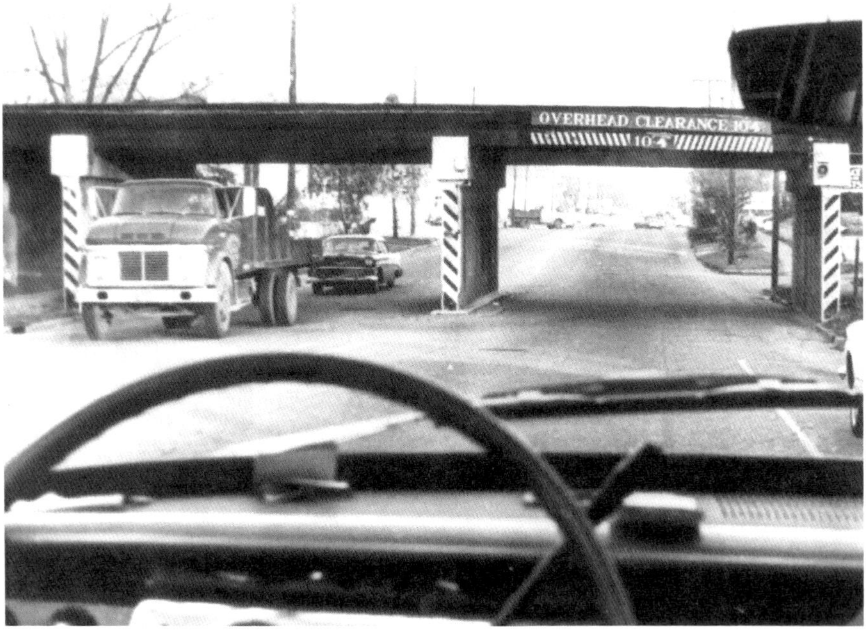

Around the time of World War I, an underpass was built on Cheves Street between the 100 and 200 blocks to allow traffic to move when long Atlantic Coast Line freight trains blocked downtown crossings. Its clearance was ten feet, four inches, plenty at the time. However, over the years, trucks became bigger and began to hit the rail bed. It became known as "the needle's eye," and despite warning lights and other measures, collisions became more and more frequent. Finally, in the 1970s, it was rebuilt and things have been better since, though sometimes it floods. *Courtesy of Sonny Smith.*

which switches could be controlled for trains arriving or leaving to or from the south. Improved communications and switching capability replaced it.

Possibly the least known of Florence's landmarks was the old bridge that took the Seaboard Railroad line from Pamplico over the Atlantic Coast Line yards east of downtown. It was a cantilever bridge with two spans but was hidden from the most traveled streets by trees and grading, so many people never even knew that it was there. The most impressive landmark we ever had, it came down after the ACL and Seaboard merged.

Then there was Chase Park, which was on the east side of McQueen Street and south side of Cheves, in an "L" around a Masonic temple at the corner. Chase Park had playground equipment, some benches and shrubbery and was the only downtown park. It now is the site of a parking garage and parking lot.

This does not include the very nice houses abutting the downtown that have disappeared. Demolished have been solid business blocks on Evans, Dargan and Cheves Streets, very likely more than still stand.

One thing that's gone that few people miss is the old parking meters.

A few blocks out Oakland Avenue, from 1939 to the 1970s, was the old American Legion Stadium. The WPA built it with a nice covered grandstand and an enclosed walkway underneath for concessions and restrooms. Major League baseball exhibitions were played there, and once a minor league ball club called it home. Lack of maintenance doomed it.

Harllee (Park) School, Holmes School, old Wilson High and the old Belk and Sear's buildings went down, and others are now in jeopardy. We've lost a lot downtown, but we have gained many parking places. They are usually vacant, but there they are.

If all of these things in or on the edge of the downtown could be resurrected, they could make a pretty impressive town.

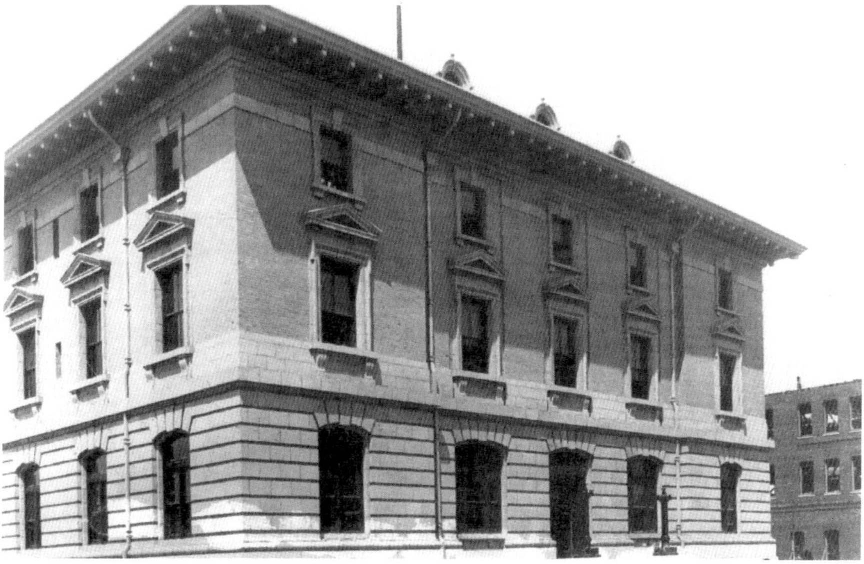

The old post office and federal building at Irby and Evans Streets was nearing completion in 1906 when this picture was taken. It housed not only postal services but also federal court and other federal offices until the new John L. McMillan Federal Building was occupied in the 1970s, two blocks west on Evans. A new main post office went up at Evans and Cashua, and the old post office went into private hands. At the right is the store building on the northeast corner of Evans and Irby that was under construction at the same time as the post office and also still stands in 2009. *Courtesy of Wayne King.*

About the Author

Thom Anderson is a native and lifelong resident of Florence except for time spent away during college and army service. He is a graduate of McClenaghan High School and the University of South Carolina and attended The Citadel and Francis Marion University. He spent about forty years in South Carolina journalism, mostly at the *Morning News*, where he frequently wrote columns telling stories about things that occurred in Florence's past. He was co-author of an earlier book that dealt with World War II veterans from Florence County.

In 1959, he and Sandra Ann Nofal, also of Florence, married. They have two sons, Mark and Kyle, daughter-in-law Jill W. Anderson and granddaughters Brittany and Katelyn White.